ISABEL VERSTRAETE

THE CARE PRINCIPLES

LEADERSHIP PLAYBOOK

I kid you not

20 STEPS TO ENGAGE DIVERSE AND MULTIGENERATIONAL TEAMS

Lannoo Campus

CONTENTS

PLAY SECTION 1 — 7
WHY I CONTINUE TO ADVOCATE FOR THE CARE PRINCIPLES: A PERSONAL NOTE ON MY PURPOSE IN LIFE — 7

PLAY SECTION 2 — 17
WHAT IS THE CARE PRINCIPLES STRATEGIC FRAMEWORK AND HOW IS IT APPLIED IN LEADERSHIP? — 17
    What are the CARE Principles? — 17
    The CARE leadership model - 20 steps to empower your diverse and multigenerational teams — 20
    Why the current leadership style needs an update — 24

PLAY SECTION 3 — 33
FIGHTING AGAINST CONSERVATIVE POWERS AND OUTDATED IDEAS — 33
    6 work-floor challenges in leading multigenerational teams — 34
    Why many leaders resist change — 43
    Podcast interview with Bart van Olphen, Founder and CEO at Fish Tales — 51

PLAY SECTION 4 — 55
THE MULTIGENERATIONAL WORKFORCE IS TODAY'S REALITY — 55
    What is a multigenerational workforce? — 55
    Podcast interview with Ali E. Cevik, founder and CEO HR-ON — 68

PLAY SECTION 5 — 71
COLLABORATION IS FUNDAMENTAL — 71

- Possible Collaboration hurdles — 72
- Care Scan tool: discover your organizational flaws and where to start CARE — 73
- The 5 steps of successful Collaboration — 73
- 🎙 **Podcast interview** with Erik-Jan Mares, CEO Zeeman — 93
- Collaboration exercises — 95

PLAY SECTION 6 — 99
AGILITY IS NEEDED — 99

- Possible Agility hurdles — 102
- How agile are organizations? The CARE Scan benchmark study reveals — 103
- The 5 steps to demonstrate Agility in leadership — 104
- 🎙 **Podcast interview** with Hanan Challouki, founder of Inclusified and Hijabs at Work — 126
- Agility exercises — 128

PLAY SECTION 7 — 135
RELIABILITY IS ESSENTIAL — 135

- Reliability hurdles — 136
- Are organizations reliable? — 139
- The 5 steps to be(come) a reliable leader — 140
- 🎙 **Podcast interview** with Professor Andreas Rasche, Professor and Associate Dean at Copenhagen Business School — 156
- Reliability exercises — 158

PLAY SECTION 8 — 163
EMPATHY MATTERS — 163

- Empathy hurdles — 166
- What does the benchmark study on the CARE Principles reveal? — 171
- The 5 essential steps of Empathy — 172
- 🎙 **Podcast interview** with Professor Anita Nowak, award-winning educator at McGill University Canada — 187
- Empathy exercises — 189

PLAY SECTION 9 **193**
THERE IS NO CARE WITHOUT SELF-CARE – A FINAL WORD
ON HOW TRANSFORMATION STARTS WITHIN **193**
- Podcast interview: Matthias Lauwers, yoga teacher 198

THANK YOU **199**
ABOUT ISABEL VERSTRAETE **203**
ENDNOTES **205**

PLAY SECTION 1

WHY I CONTINUE TO ADVOCATE FOR THE CARE PRINCIPLES: A PERSONAL NOTE ON MY PURPOSE IN LIFE

I must have been 5 years old when I was singing 'Pour un flirt avec toi' from Michel Delpech[1] in my grandfather's small workers' house. It was our favourite song to dance and sing along to, although I had no clue that the French text was about flirting. My grandfather predicted there and then that I would have an international career as an entertainer. I forgot about this childhood memory for almost five decades, and singing has never been my skill, but my grandfather's predictive powers have somehow come true as I engage with international business crowds through strategic work, podcast interviews, and keynote sessions.

Writing this second book made me wonder, am I an entertainer? I surely never considered myself one, but some introspection made me realise that my life has profoundly changed since I wrote my first book, *'Does your brand CARE? Building a better world with the CARE Principles'*. Being at the forefront of change, inspiring business leaders and showing them opportunities rather than challenges might not be a classic interpretation of an entertainer, but it somehow fits my mission. Both my personal life and my business career have shifted tremendously. My book led to the discovery of my true purpose, and that is to show organizations and leaders that commercial success is possible when combined with CARE for people and the planet. Choosing for a People –

Planet – Prosperity model is a model to become future-fit; it's just a matter of making the effort to choose for transitioning now.

The past few years made me realise that we live in challenging times; we can no longer sit back and wait for others to solve the issues we see. We need to take some kind of responsibility; we need to use our voices to speak up publicly. We need to say no to injustice, racism, narcissistic leaders and abusive power in any form. We need to choose now to be part of the solution, and no longer remain part of the problem. So maybe it is my destiny to be an advocate for change, an author, a public speaker, a podcast host, and a passionate warrior for more caring and sustainable leadership… However when my book emerged during the Covid-19 lockdowns in 2021, I had no clue about any of this.

My job as a brand strategist was on hold due to the pandemic, my business partnership ended and expectations as a first-time author were modest at best. Little did I anticipate the transformative journey this book would set me on, and it all started with one person: Professor Jos Rath, a purpose marketer and Associate Professor of Philanthropy at the Vrije University in Amsterdam. Jos reached out to me on LinkedIn and praised my CARE framework as a teaching methodology. Considering I hadn't attended university myself, a message from a professor on LinkedIn felt like a prank. To my surprise, Jos was serious, marking a pivotal moment that led to a guest lecture at VU Amsterdam. Top marketer and ex-client of mine Rene Repko also showed enthusiasm and introduced me to Professor Henry Robben of Nyenrode Business University. Henry, now a big fan and ally of the CARE Principles, consistently invites me to lecture at his MBA training at Nyenrode.

These kinds of experiences became the foundation not only for guest lectures at respected institutions like VU Amsterdam, TU Delft, Vlerick Brussels and more, but also encouraged me to delve further into public speaking, to become a trained keynote speaker. Without a career change in mind, I evolved from a brand strategist who presents plans to management teams to a keynote speaker who entertains international business and student audiences – even occasionally dancing with my audiences on stage. Engaging with such diverse audiences, from young students to seasoned professionals, provided invaluable insights, and revealed a small but impactful group of people of all ages, eager to drive positive change and wanting to make an impact. Simultaneously, I launched a podcast featuring insightful conversations with leaders from the public and private sectors (inter)national. Their willingness to share how they apply CARE – Collaboration, Agility, Reliability, and Empathy – in their organizations taught me how ahead they are of their competitors. How their attention to a caring culture, a sustainable approach to growth, and an urge to experiment with working in new and different ways was truly transformational for their organizations.

In retrospect, the launch of the CARE Principles seemed successful, but transparency obliges me to say that it appeals mostly to the innovators and early birds, the seekers and atypical leaders who have no problem with daring to try out new things. Today that group remains a small group. I comprehend that most business leaders talk about Profit, People and Planet, but are mainly concerned about Profit. The concept of People – Planet – Prosperity has not yet landed in many leaders' goals. Some are ready on a personal level, but are held back by their board of directors or other shareholders. I have realised that most people ignore today's challenges – probably a coping mechanism for the hard world we live in. I feel the conservative powers of leadership have little to no real care for people and the planet. I see a world in which many people escape in disengagement and entertainment in diverse forms from endless scrolls through cat videos to avoiding news, and not daring to open their mouth when they witness toxic and unacceptable behaviour in any form.

We continue to see how the media perpetuates a narrative of conservatism and populism, how global CO_2 emissions continue to rise, and how social change remains insufficient. Many corporate practices have reverted to pre-pandemic norms, ignoring the leadership needs of younger and more diverse generations. At the same time, recent studies[2] reveal how employee disengagement levels are the highest in a decade. In 2024 global research from Gallup[3] indicated that employee engagement is as low as 23%. Certain companies see their growth plans jeopardised as they lose as much talent as they hire. Burnout numbers continue to climb, and although burnout is not solely linked to work environments, most research sees a link between this disease and the way employees are treated at work.

There is ample proof from Forbes, Deloitte, Gallup, and other leading voices in business that organizations who care thrive:

- In the most successful companies, employee engagement is as high as 72%.[4]
- Organizations without burnt out people make 40% more profit[5].
- Companies with a true purpose grow three times faster than their competitors, while achieving higher customer and employee satisfaction[6].
- Moreover, having a strong purpose creates trust. Consumers[7] are 4.1 times more likely to trust a company when they think it has a strong purpose.
- Highly engaged teams show 21% greater profitability.
- With engaged teams, organizations realise a 41% reduction in absenteeism.[8]

These findings suggest that integrating purpose and care into business strategies not only contributes to societal benefits, but also enhances business performance by connecting more deeply with employees and consumers who prioritise ethical and sustainable practices.

> **Good leaders build products.**
> **Great leaders build cultures.**
>
> **Good leaders deliver results.**
> **Great leaders develop people.**
>
> **Good leaders have vision.**
> **Great leaders have values.**
>
> **ADAM GRANT, AMERICAN PSYCHOLOGIST, AUTHOR, AND PROFESSOR**

Despite the evidence that leadership and the way we treat people needs to be revised, in my job I witness a sense of widespread dissatisfaction and a lack of understanding between both leaders and employees. Many leaders still seem to think people can be squeezed even more to attain the objectives of eternal growth. The pressure on people is huge, even on those in the highest ranks.

A CEO told me that even when he was very ill in bed, his zoom calls with his international bosses continued. His bosses did not care that he was ill; the business had to continue, no mercy! Many leaders believe that rules, duty, and listening to the boss is the only way to steer teams. I hear many complaints from CEOs who tell me they have no clue how to keep Millennials on board. In some sectors, it has reached a point where organizations face growth obstacles. A lack of gaining and/or retaining talent prevents them from growing their business. This is not only the case in the tourist and hospitality industry; in the healthcare, technology, manufacturing, and construction sectors there is also a need for more talent. A lack of understanding of how to deal with younger and diverse generations creates frustration for everyone inside organizations. I witness leadership flaws, multigenerational teams who fail to collaborate, bureaucratic processes, poor communication skills, and huge trust and comprehension issues. Combine this with a lack of purpose, and the speed of technological revolutions such as artificial intelligence, and you understand the fear and fatigue among employees and leaders alike.

Frankly, I could have chosen to wait for the new generations to take over, but patience is not my biggest talent. So, I decided – not really planned – to write a second book to share how to apply the CARE Principles in leadership. My experience helped me to realise that before we can place CARE at the core of a business strategy, we need to place CARE at the core of the hearts of leaders. We need to convince the leaders of today to work differently with the diverse and multigenerational workforce of today and tomorrow. I realised that I need to shift my focus from brand strategist to people strategist, as it is the people who block the growth of their own organizations, starting with the leadership teams who need a new set of skills to engage their teams. Imagine how your organization could grow and thrive if you managed to work with your people and not against them! To engage, involve, empower, and inspire them so they thrive, learn, enjoy work, and bring sustainable growth to the organization.

The simple quote 'If you change, the world changes' haunts me in a positive way. The death of both my parents – since my previous book was published – has probably given me an even fiercer drive to act and use my skills and voice. The conservative powers who try to hold back change, the paternalistic leaders who want to have women back in supportive roles, the polarising leaders who prefer war to peace are my fuel to fight back. My reach might not be that big, but it should not hold me back from trying to make this world a better place. I want to continue to use my voice and modest reach to preach for change, openness, mildness, and care. Not only for my own mental health, but for my daughters' future too.

Trends, like horses, are easier to ride in the direction they are going.

THOMAS GEUKEN, ASSOCIATE DIRECTOR, COPENHAGEN INSTITUTE FOR FUTURE STUDIES

I experienced how one person can have a serious impact on your life: Jos Rath changed my destiny forever. I hope to impact your life too. I urge you to start using your voice. We can all make this world a better place; that is a fact. We can no longer wait for others to do it for us; we must step up and start a revolution ourselves. No time to waste – life is short, as you will see in the next exercise – and as I mentioned before, the CARE Principles made me discover my own purpose. We all have transformative powers; it is just a question of realising this and embracing the much-needed transformation to become a better version of yourself.

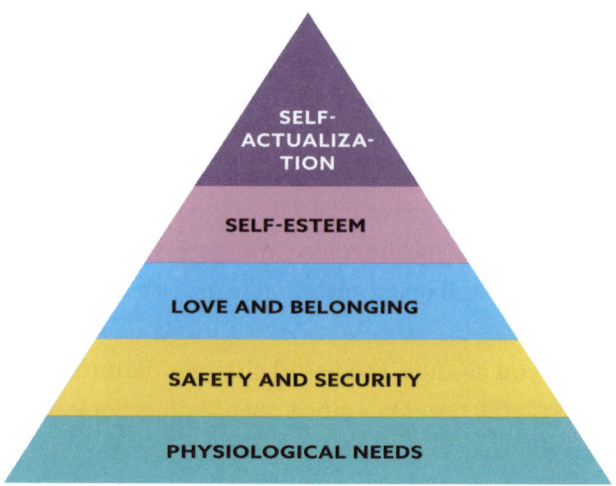

Figure 1: Maslow's Hierarchy of Needs.

We all know that the highest level in Maslow's hierarchy of needs is self-actualisation – the desire to become the best that one can be. It is less well known that he added a level shortly before his death. This level is the highest level of human need – self-transcendence. The focus shifts from self-fulfilment to the well-being of others. This stage is about connecting to something larger than oneself and helping others to achieve their potential. That is the reason I want you to become the best IN and FOR the world. To do this, we must challenge the traditional codes of success and leadership. Embracing a positive mindset, practising inclusiveness and care, and daring to collaborate are essential. We must be confident enough to pioneer unconventional paths, remain agile, and demonstrate empathy. Dare to be vulnerable and learn how to stay curious to understand others. Embrace our female traits to nurture and care more for people and the planet. Finally, in a world soon to be dominated by fast-learning machines and where a lot of fake images but also fake news is being spread, humans must protect their reliable status and define their moral compass.

How you can do this is the purpose of this leadership playbook and CARE Principles model! This playbook offers you a step-by-step approach to follow, or not. A playbook full of inspiration of caring leaders. A playbook full of exercises, carefully crafted by the talented Dutch purpose coach Mette Visser.[9] Mette was also a CARE Principles supporter at the very start, and she was the perfect ally to bring my methodology alive with practical, hands-on exercises for all! We had fun selecting and crafting the best exercises; we hope you learn in a playful way how to become a better leader too. Don't miss the podcast episode in which she explains why she cares. This playbook is no fluffy soft-skills oriented blah-blah-blah approach; it is a 20-step process to lead your teams to higher performance, more engagement, true empowerment, sky-high productivity, increased revenue and, above all, happier teams. Because let's face it, when we feel happy, we can take on the world! This book is called a playbook. That is no coincidence because the definition of a playbook is a collection of strategies that a team trusts to execute their job. It is used to ensure consistency and effectiveness in achieving goals.

I hope you see this playbook as a collection of strategies that stimulates you to see work as a playful activity, something to be done with energy and fun, in co-creation and with loads of trust in and curiosity about the ideas of others.

I hope to inspire you to let go of the idea of command and control, to go with the flow and experience how you can rise above yourself, if you let others help you. As we embark on a quest to spread more CARE for a positive, constructive, and sustainable future, the call goes out to game-changers, trailblazers, daredevils, innovators, and seekers to stand up and take responsibility, ushering in a new era of leadership! Are you ready to break free from outdated leadership paradigms and inspire all generations in your teams? Or do you want to continue to burn money with your non-engaged workforce? The choice is yours to transform yourself and your organization for the better!

Expressing gratitude for those embracing lifelong learning, criticism, vulnerability, discomfort, and teamwork – attributes demanded by different generations – I thank you for becoming one of these leaders. This book is a tribute to the many leaders of tomorrow I have met and who have embraced the CARE Principles. Each chapter introduces you to the inspiring leaders who have made a difference in their unique ways. Each chapter offers exercises to get you going, so today you can start your own transformation. Achieving excellence IN and FOR the world is not a dream, it is a reality! Check it out – see how it can become your reality too!

Finally, care and self-care didn't come naturally to me; I learned it the hard way, unfortunately, and will share more about my own transformative journey throughout this book. Xander De Bouw, my personal trainer, and Matthias Lauwers, my yoga teacher, have helped me tremendously to better understand myself, connect my head to my body, and slow down my pace more often, to have enough energy for this long-haul journey I started of trying to make this world a better place.

Thank you and take care,
Isabel

PS: This book has been written by me with the help of Chat GPT4!

EXERCISE

Kick-start your personal transformation

While we are all so busy with work, obligations, family and chasing welfare and financial growth, it is quite revealing to read the top five regrets people have when they are facing their own mortality. Bronnie Ware,[10] an Australian palliative carer, collected her patients' regrets.

The top five regrets are:
1. I wish I'd had the courage to live a life true to myself, not the life others expected of me.
2. I wish I hadn't worked so hard.
3. I wish I'd had the courage to express my feelings.
4. I wish I had stayed in touch with my friends.
5. I wish that I had let myself be happier.

So, stop for a second, take a piece of paper and dare to ask yourself the following questions:
1. What are you doing here on earth?
2. To make this question even more relevant, dare to calculate how much remaining time you have left in your life. Think about it and recognise that your time is limited as you can try out yourself on a scary death calculator like this one: https://deathcalculator.ai/
3. Imagine what people will say about you at your funeral. Will they only talk about your financial gains, houses, and fancy cars you proudly showed off?
4. Will they talk about how you made a difference?

Scary, right? I know! The death calculator freaked me out too, I kid you not, but it also made me appreciate that I have no time to waste, and I must focus on my purpose in life! So, let's dive straight into the CARE Principles strategic framework so you can get started!

Collaboration

Agility

Reliability

Empathy

PLAY SECTION 2

WHAT IS THE CARE PRINCIPLES STRATEGIC FRAMEWORK AND HOW IS IT APPLIED IN LEADERSHIP?

WHAT ARE THE CARE PRINCIPLES?

Showing you care for others is always a good start and might already differentiate you from other leaders. However, developing the CARE Principles on a deeper level can help you truly empower all generations on the work floor. Applying the four Principles of collaboration, agility, reliability, and empathy is always done in a unique mix that fits best with you and your company's DNA.

The ability to adapt your leadership team's behaviour in becoming a more collaborative, agile, reliable, and empathic version of themselves will take time. Applying these Principles entails a profound adaptation of your organization, your structure, your processes, your attitude, and your way of thinking. This framework offers you a step-by-step process to turn around your leadership skills and processes.

It is important to understand why these four Principles matter and why they need to be accelerated. As mentioned in my first book, I really dislike the term 'human resources', a term that seems to have been developed in an era when the human part didn't really matter and employees were considered just another resource to be exploited, like financial or natural resources... So, throughout this book I will use the term 'your people' or 'your talent', because frankly they are more than just another 'resource' for making your business successful! The complete CARE strategic framework is built to go beyond your talent; the framework reaches out to your clients, stakeholders, and CARE for the planet too.

As this book is about internal leadership skills and processes, we won't focus on the client – stakeholder – planet part, which doesn't mean that leadership is not to be shown in those domains! Showing leadership is also about collaborating in an open and transparent way with your suppliers, your government, your neighbours, your competitors – in short, with all external stakeholders. Finally, all leadership must be done in the most sustainable way; frugality is the only way forward. Just as everything in our globalised world is interconnected, so it is with your business too. You can have the best staff ever and be the most award-winning employer of modern times, but if you do not take care of your clients, you won't last. But the CARE Principles really start internally as your employees are your number one ambassador and your leadership teams have a huge effect on how your organization treats them. So, in this book we focus on internal leadership and our leadership model is crafted to engage diverse and multigenerational teams, a reality on most work floors. More on that topic later.

Before you read on, I would like you to stop for a second and think about your inner child. We were taught to give up the kid inside us when we became adults. Adulthood is serious and play is something we might occasionally do with our children. We do not associate play with work. But I challenge you to revise your opinion on this, therefore this book is called a playbook. In the Industrial Age, playfulness has always been suppressed; we have to be mature and serious to succeed. Today, as more and more jobs in the production and service industries will be automated, the creative industries will grow. Our human imagination and playfulness will become increasingly important parameters for success. It might become our biggest advantage compared to generative AI! When we allow play, joy, fun, trial, and error, it will bring us into flow. I will get back to this in the Collaboration Play Section. So, when you read on, see the next 20 steps as something to play with, to enjoy yourself with, to be surprised by in the exercises we crafted for you. Like anything in life, some will work for you, others won't. That is okay! Simply understand that to drive better employee engagement, and have stronger ties, it is important to create a culture that is fun and allows playfulness for all.

Your people

Your clients

Your stakeholders

The planet

THE CARE LEADERSHIP MODEL
20 STEPS TO EMPOWER YOUR DIVERSE

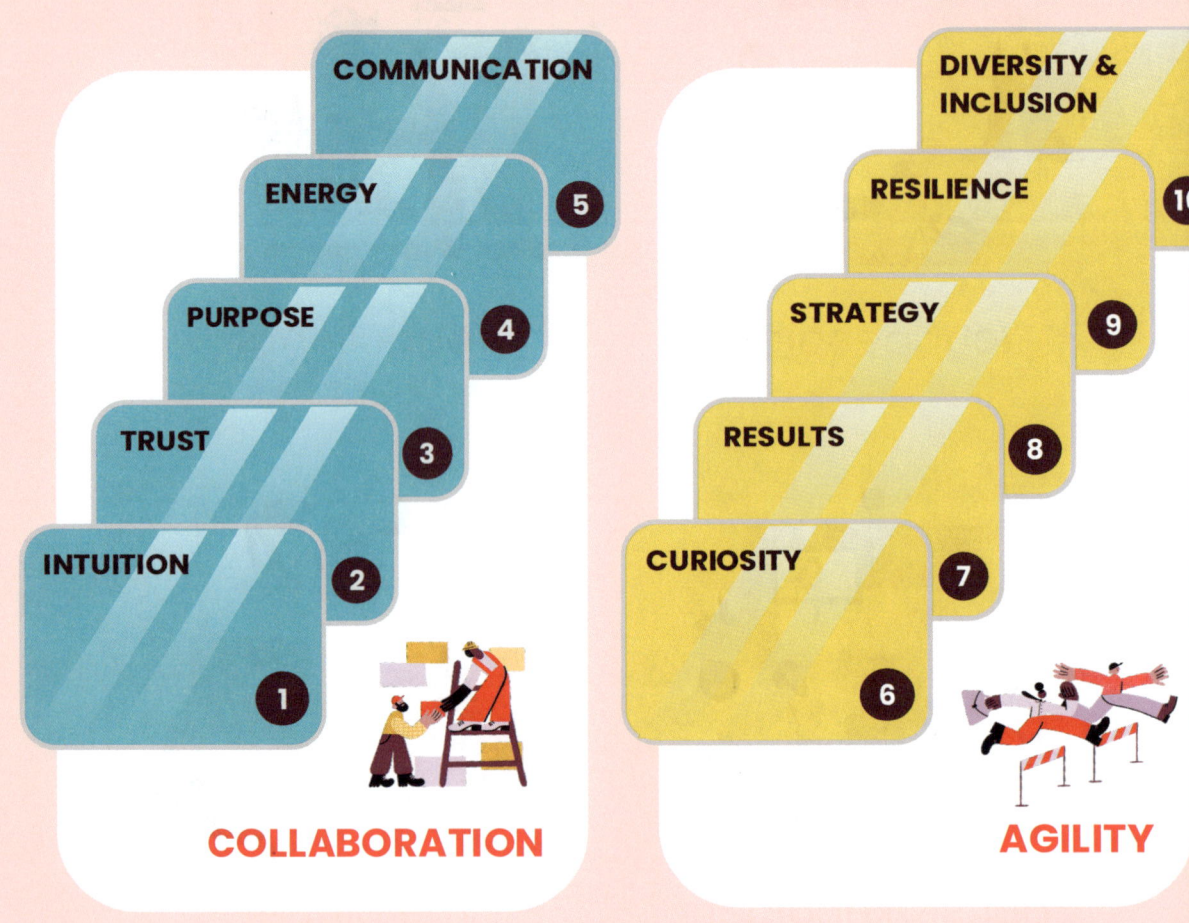

AND MULTIGENERATIONAL TEAMS

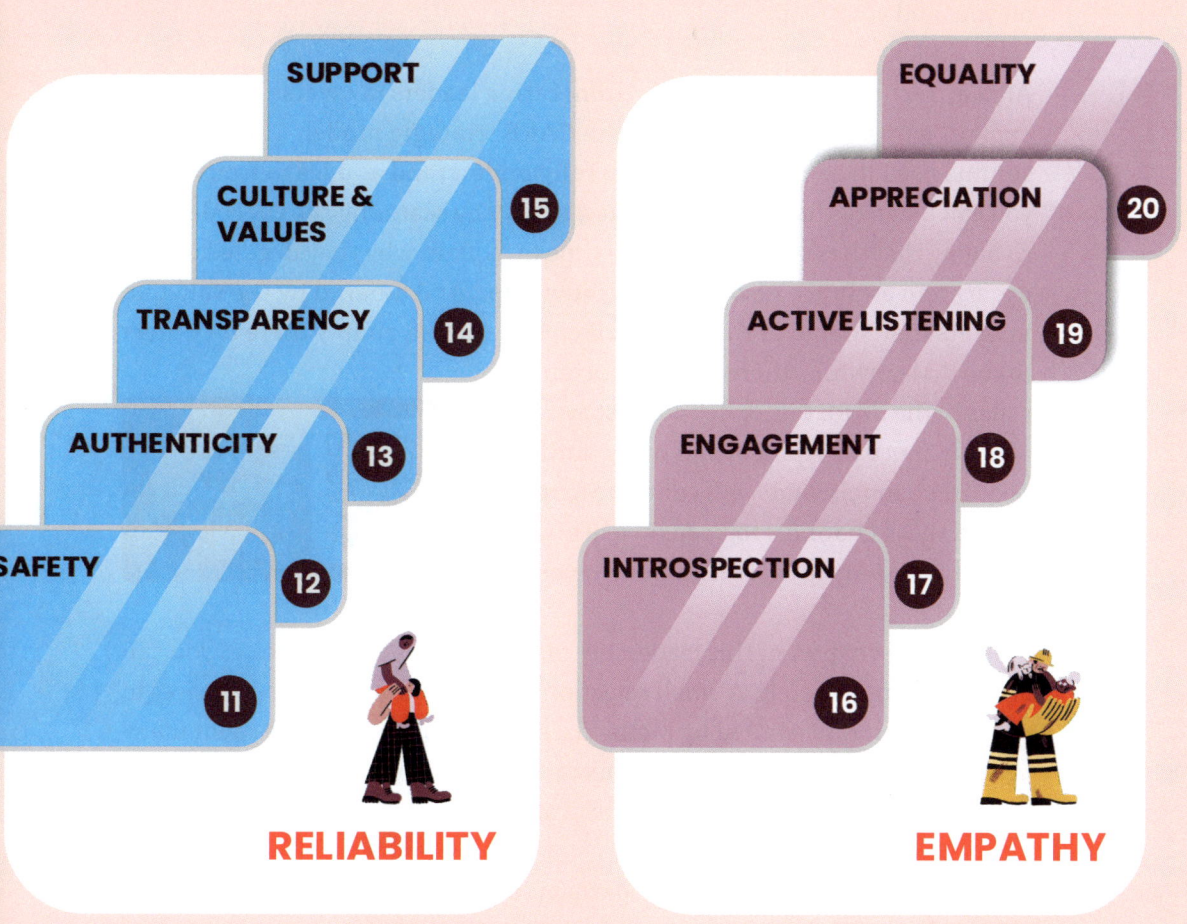

Have a look at the 20 steps within the CARE Leadership model. I know, 20 steps seem a whole lot, but don't worry; we tried to split the transition process into a step-by-step approach, so it is accessible to all. Note that you don't need to follow these 20 steps in this order. If you believe your biggest issues lie in the empathy field, jump straight into that play section and exercises. If you know your instinct and intuition are fine, skip this step and dive straight into the trust issue. This is a playbook, and we hope you find pleasure in playing with it and enjoy the transformational power it will have on you, and your team.

All play sections bring inspiration from caring leaders in diverse sectors who explain why and how they apply the CARE strategic model. Their tips are summarised in each chapter, but to fully understand and learn from them, you can listen to the podcast interview simply by scanning the QR code. I am so happy that these leaders took the time to explain why they decided to step up, act and embrace new codes of leadership. And amazed by the valuable insights they shared in the CARE Principles podcast, simply there for others to copy! Meanwhile, there are over 100 episodes in the CARE Principles podcast available on Spotify,[11] Apple,[12] and other audio podcast channels, and I will continue to invest in these channels to keep on learning myself and sharing that wisdom with you.

Scan here to listen to the CARE Principles podcast.

Finally, each chapter of this leadership playbook ends with exercises you can start to do immediately. A small selection of solo, duo, and group exercises to get going, carefully crafted by Mette Visser, a purpose coach who spent many years managing teams in her previous career in fashion. As Mette's mum is an experienced coach, she learned the drill at her mother's knee.

Does leadership need an update and what is expected from leaders today? Read on to understand the scope of transformation demanded by more diverse and multigenerational teams.

WHY THE CURRENT LEADERSHIP

COLLABORATION

1. From COMMAND to INTUITION
2. From CONTROL to TRUST
3. From DUTY to PURPOSE
4. From APATHY to ENERGY
5. From MONOLOGUE to DIALOGUE

AGILITY

6. From KNOWLEDGE to CURIOSITY
7. From TIME to RESULTS
8. From PLANNING to STRATEGY
9. From FRAGILITY to RESILIENCE
10. From EXCLUSION to INCLUSION

STYLE NEEDS AN UPDATE

RELIABILITY

11. From FEAR to SAFETY
12. From INSINCERITY to AUTHENTICITY
13. From SECRECY to TRANSPARENCY
14. From PROCEDURES to CULTURE
15. From POWER to SUPPORT

EMPATHY

16. From EXTROSPECTION to INTROSPECTION
17. From DETACHMENT to ENGAGEMENT
18. From ORDER to ACTIVE LISTENING
19. From EVALUATION to APPRECIATION
20. From HIERARCHY to EQUALITY

In each play section, we will dive deeper into each step to explain how to do it, and why it is necessary. We will also explain some leadership hurdles, current beliefs or attitudes often spotted today among managers. To try to make it clear why a shift is needed, specifically if you want to grow your organization with a diverse and multigenerational team, I will share insights from my 20+ years' experience in broad marketing and strategic consultancy roles, completed with relevant research on the changes demanded by younger generations.

Today's leadership skills often date back to the early 20th century, like the scientific management theory introduced by Frederick W. Taylor,[13] but they won't do in the technological era we have landed in. The command-and-control leadership style characterised by a strict hierarchy and centralised decision-making process is rooted in military history and has been practised for centuries. Today many leaders still practise this style and believe that time control, a top-down approach, strict rules, and duty-focused tasks create a happy and productive workforce.

This is delusional, especially with younger people. Optimising work processes and labour productivity that is mostly in hands of robots these days doesn't need this strict supervision and control of people. However, many leaders seem stuck in leadership styles from the industrial era. I call it the CCC-syndrome that many leaders suffer from. What is the CCC-syndrome? It stands for leaders who like to:
- COMMAND
- CONTROL
- CORRECT

Why does this no longer work?
- **Changing workforce expectations:** Millennials (people born between 1981 and 1996) and Generation Z (people born between 1997 and 2012) value autonomy, purpose, and work-life balance more than previous generations. The authoritative nature of command and control does not satisfy their needs, leading to decreased employee engagement and lower retention.
- **Bureaucratic and slow processes can lead to a competitive disadvantage:** Work today is often more complex, requiring multidisciplinary knowledge and collaboration across departments and geographies. The

top-down approach of command and control can hinder the flow of information and collaboration needed to tackle complex challenges effectively.
- **Cultural and social laws:** Society is constantly changing and evolving, whether we like it or not. There's been a broad cultural shift towards valuing transparency, accountability, and ethical leadership. Business environments where decision-making is opaque and feedback loops are limited are considered outdated.
- **Lifelong learning, innovation and adaptation are key:** In this technological era, groundbreaking technologies such as artificial intelligence, robotics, blockchain, Internet of Things, quantum computing, and regenerative thinking, to name a few technological disruptions, will completely impact the way we work. Lifelong learning and constant training and educating of the workforce will be needed to remain relevant. Leaders will work with new generations of youngsters who are born with a skillset they don't master. Trust, respect, a result-driven approach, and dialogue will be key to keep that generation happy and engaged. Collaborative and inclusive leadership styles are better suited to fostering innovation. All research proves that.

This is reason enough to adapt our leadership style, but honesty obliges me to say that it not only comes with learning how to embrace the new. The CARE Principles leadership also comes with more equality, leaving you a less privileged spot at the table. Visiting companies, I can immediately see the organizational culture and leadership style by the parking and the way the receptionist receives me. Parking spots reserved close to the entrance generally means the organization is traditional and the bosses like everyone to see their privilege. If receptionists are kind and warm, you immediately feel a caring and warm culture. If receptionists hardly look at you, and wave to the machines where you need to type in your name, you can bet that organization has a command-and-control type of leadership.

I understand that the informal perks of current leaders are often a reward for their responsibilities and stress. Bigger cars, better parking spots, a fancy executive restaurant to lunch in, and other perks are reserved for those at the top of the ladder. In the office of a big coffee brand, the management even had access to better coffee, I kid you not. Blue-collar and white-collar employees who did not work on the executive floor were left with horrible machine coffee that tasted like dishwater, while the management had access to freshly ground

I kid you not

coffee beans and steamed milk for their cappuccinos. While the people who made the coffee in the factory had the worst quality cup, the leaders savoured the finest selection of beans, made in the best conditions. True story! Giving most of your privileges up for a more collaborative and equal management style where everybody matters and deserves a good cup of coffee seems easy, right? Well, you will see that old habits are often difficult to let go of. Everybody loves privileges and becoming equals in treatment can be scary.

> **Leadership is not about being in charge. It's about taking care of those in your charge.**
>
> **SIMON SINEK**

However, we promise that although you might have to walk a bit further to your company car – but hey, walking is healthy! – you will also be rewarded in so many other ways by your engaged and empowered team, and that will make up for all the informal perks you once enjoyed! But transforming the current leadership style is not only about giving up the C-level perks. It is about the hard facts of growth, profit, competitive advantage, innovation and building the foundations now for a long-term existence. To keep your business healthy and thriving you need talent. Have a look at recent research and the staggering truth of employees today. The biggest wake-up call you can get is the rise in workforce disengagement, raising levels of stress and dissatisfaction of people at work.

The U.S. research and advisory firm Gallup[14] researched this topic and gathered the following data in 2024:
- 77% of the global workforce does not feel engaged at work.
- 59% of employees are quiet quitting. In Europe this number rises to 72%!
- 51% of employees are on the look-out for a new job.
- 44% of employees feel a lot of stress at work. In Europe this number is 39%.
- 37% believe their job makes no useful contribution to society.
- 34% of an annual salary is the cost of disengagement.
- 18% of employees are loud quitting. In Europe this number is a bit lower, at 15%!

How can we keep our teams motivated, drive energy and kick-start trust? Global research is not the only source of worrying statistics; in the academic world, there are also voices pleading for a new kind of leadership. Rune Todnem By is a Professor of Leadership and the UNESCO Chair on Leadership, Innovation, and Anticipation at the University of Stavanger, Norway. He published an academic paper[15] about leadership and purpose. Professor Rath asked his students to read it before my CARE Principles guest lecture at the VU Amsterdam in 2023. Of course, I read it too and got so enthusiastic about his vision! As this academic paper is too long to summarise here, I would like to share his EPICally MAD leadership model – a model designed to inspire and guide leaders towards making a significant, positive impact within their organizations and society at large. The acronym EPICally MAD stands for Ethical, Purposeful, Impactful, and Courageous leadership that Makes A Difference. You can watch this inspirational Norwegian professor's TED Talk on YouTube[16] if you are curious!

Leadership convention is outdated and in urgent need of a much-required update. What the globe, society, and organizations within need is a united rather than fragmented development of leadership theory and practice moving forward. If we are to stand any chance of delivering on the UN's SDGs and other complex challenges lying ahead of us, we simply can't continue relying on what is an outdated leadership convention designed to deliver external goods (e.g. power, influence, wealth, and status as ends in themselves) to the detriment of what is best for most.

RUNE TODNEM BY, PROFESSOR OF LEADERSHIP AND UNESCO CHAIR ON LEADERSHIP, INNOVATION, AND ANTICIPATION AT THE UNIVERSITY OF STAVANGER, NORWAY

I can only align with this professor as I am convinced from my experiences that we need a fresh view on leadership and how today's leaders steer their teams! Leading people in these challenging times will demand:

- A choice for partnerships and collaboration.
- A sense of agility and flexibility to be able to adapt ourselves to the constantly changing reality we face.
- Trust and reliability – key for all human relationships.
- Empathy, compassion, and simply embracing a softer side of oneself – crucial to engaging in real conversations, authentic bonding, and true connection.
- A focus on having a purpose. This is essential to all leadership conversations and practice.
- Being open to diversity and inclusion – necessary to invite more people to the table and involve them on all levels of the conversation.
- Making work environments safe spaces where people can be themselves. This is crucial for maximum engagement and higher performance.
- A fairer distribution of power, influence, wealth and status and a pursuit of greater equality that starts within teams.
- Building mental resilience and ways of self-care to avoid being burdened by stress and anxiety. This is key for everyone.

More real-life examples of leadership dos and don'ts are coming up, but before we get going and learn progressively how to apply CARE leadership, let's look at the many and fast changes around you, and how they will demand new leadership skills.

PLAY SECTION 3

FIGHTING AGAINST CONSERVATIVE POWERS AND OUTDATED IDEAS

Let's face it, today's world is not easy. We are on the brink of a poly-crisis, a word for the multitude of crises we are going through: economic, social, political, technological, geopolitical, health, and climate just to name some of the most dominant crises we feel today. Pulitzer Prize winner and New York Times columnist Thomas Friedman[17] argues that we are in the middle of three giant accelerations – changes involving globalisation, the earth's climate, and technology.

These changes are reshaping social and economic life in powerful ways and putting a premium on 'learning faster and governing and operating smarter'. These transformative forces in markets, climate, and technology are 'melting into one giant change'. In this interconnected giant change, there is a clear call for a new kind of leadership, a new approach.

> **Making money is for some people no longer enough, they want to start making meaning.**
>
> **UNKNOWN**

The traditional, macho-style leader, clinging to hierarchy and egocentric behaviour, is losing touch with the evolving demands of the younger and more diverse generations. Still, conservative powers are strong and fighting back harder, it seems, to cling onto their power. Many people are afraid of change and hope to stick to what they know and what they have. We also witness an uplift of conservatism[18] among all age groups, and liberal ideas and political parties are under pressure. Specifically, boys[19] tend to choose more traditional and conservative values, compared to girls. In hindsight, society in general is getting more progressive and democratic, but many people seem overwhelmed by the many and fast changes in society, and therefore some of them tend to hold on to the known, more traditional, and conservative values.

Now there are many good things to say about traditional values like trust, honesty, duty, and respect, but when we go back to the topic of leadership, we need an update, the leader who suffers from the CCC-syndrome no longer does it. Younger generations demand to work in a different and more flexible way, and talent is reshaping the world of work-learn-play-live modus as interconnected aspects of life, as work is no longer seen as something separate from private lives. Redesigning work trends started before Covid, but the global pandemic has pushed through certain new realities. Discussions on when, why, as well as where we work, need to be massively re-assessed. These discussions will impact leadership for sure, but also the shape, size, and function of our offices. We need to address the issues of diverse and different generations and find an answer to why people are resigning from their work without alternatives in place. This is why. Let me share the six biggest challenges we see on today's work floor.

6 WORK-FLOOR CHALLENGES IN LEADING MULTIGENERATIONAL TEAMS

- **Younger generations are part of the leadership team.**

Due to their digital and technological skills, younger people show up more often in leadership positions today, compared to the past. In the past, climbing the career ladder was based on skills for sure, but also on experience and age. You rarely met management members of 30 years old. Today you find more and more of these younger generations being part of management teams. The days in which 'juniors' are treated with a 'shut up and learn' mentality are over. Traditional hierarchies and ideas about what make a good leader will continue to be challenged. Reverse mentoring will grow in popularity as younger generations bring fresh knowledge and values.

This can create friction between multi-age people on the board level and beyond, because each generation has their specific wishes and needs. The younger generations demand better work-life balance, which many older leaders consider weak. I used to work in an advertising agency as a freelancer. Most of my colleagues had no idea that I was paid by the hour. I tried to work as efficiently as possible, and went to the office only for necessary meetings. I spent little time just hanging out there, or having chats at the coffee machine. I often received remarks such as 'Are you taking the day off?' when I left the agency at 2 p.m., for instance. These remarks obviously did not come from my boss who knew I was working on an hourly rate, but from team superiors who were convinced that being a good and dedicated employee meant you stayed late at night, worked during the weekend, and even during holidays.

I freelanced for this agency for 5 years and during that time one of the managing directors – who clearly knew about my contract – told me she found it hard that I was not always visible in the agency. She acknowledged the fact that my clients were happy, the team I steered performed and my results were satisfactory. Yet, for her, I wasn't really part of the team as I appeared only when necessary. For her being a good 'soldier', as she used to call the employees, was being present. Years later, she experienced burnout and when I met her afterwards, she told me that she finally understood that my way of working was fine. Being available for work 24/7 had led her to burnout and made her understand that she needed to redefine her work-life balance. This attitude of looking different at work – even when you are passionate about your job and responsibilities – is something that comes naturally to many Millennials and Gen Z.

- **Privilege is invisible for those who have it.**

This is what I learnt in New York. Read more about this insight in the Agility chapter. I recently witnessed it myself. Right before new year I was invited to give a keynote and workshop for an insurance company. The subject was 'self-care' and the team had planned an afternoon of inspiration, followed by a Christmas party. I saw the conference room filling up with an older and quite traditional population of managers. It is always a bit scary to be in front of a large group of new people, but here I frankly wondered if they would have any interest in my thoughts on self-care. Shortly into my talk, I could sense the non-interest of a big part of the audience. As I had to give a workshop afterwards, I knew I had to do something to change the atmosphere. I speeded up my introduction of how I saw the world and dived straight into the more light and entertaining part of facts and figures on how to take care of yourself. Luckily, I added some humour and finally we ended the afternoon dancing together. Okay, I managed to drag along a big part of this crowd, but still I was disappointed in myself for not having done better.

While most attendees rushed into the Christmas party, the boss of this department told me she had trouble understanding my unconventional view on the world and had not recognised herself in the world I sketched, of disengaged employees, burnt out people, polarised media, and anxious youngsters. She ended by saying that she was relieved that I had ended my assignment on a positive note. My overall score for my performance was rated 7,33. Hmmm, what happened here? It kept me awake at night as I hate it when I don't seem to connect with my audiences. In retrospect, I understood that insurance is a traditional industry and even though it is one of the first sectors to be confronted with the changing world – think of climate change damage like wildfires or floods – it embraces conservative thinking. It made me wonder why people in general don't accept scientific proof, or remain sceptical about societal changes.

Talking to my publisher about this haunting case(!), he assured me that many people simply deny or refuse to see the changes in society. In particular, privileged people in power may not accept scientific proof about issues like climate or societal change due to a mix of vested interests, ideological beliefs, and the potential impact of necessary changes on their economic interests. Additionally, cognitive dissonance and confirmation bias can lead individuals to reject evidence that contradicts their pre-existing beliefs or interests. This experience made me realise that we are all biased and live in self-confirming bubbles. We surround ourselves with people who think, live, eat, and consume the same media. We rarely come out of this bubble to dare to truly listen to other opinions or worries. This increases polarisation, leaving less room for empathy and understanding, and frankly means missing the chance to grow as a person and as a leader. Finally, it might also be an obstacle to engaging with talent that you will need if you want to continue to grow as an organization.

■ **Employee engagement is in decline.**

Employee engagement in Europe and in the U.S. has been a topic of concern, showing signs of stagnation and decline. Various research has indicated that engagement levels among employees have remained low over the past decade. Leadership is identified as a significant factor influencing these levels, suggesting that an improvement in how organizations are led could contribute positively to employee engagement. Gallup,[20] a leading voice in workplace performance, followed up on the state of employee engagement. Their research in the U.S. in 2024[21] indicates that since the pandemic they have witnessed a higher percentage of engagement of Baby Boomers. However, overall employee engagement is below 2020 levels!

Specifically, alarming numbers of detachment from work are noted among the younger generations. The disengagement starts with Generation X employees, but the most dramatic decline in engagement has occurred among some of the older Millennials, more specifically those born between 1980 and 1988. This age group shows higher rates of disengagement compared to younger Millennials and Generation Z.

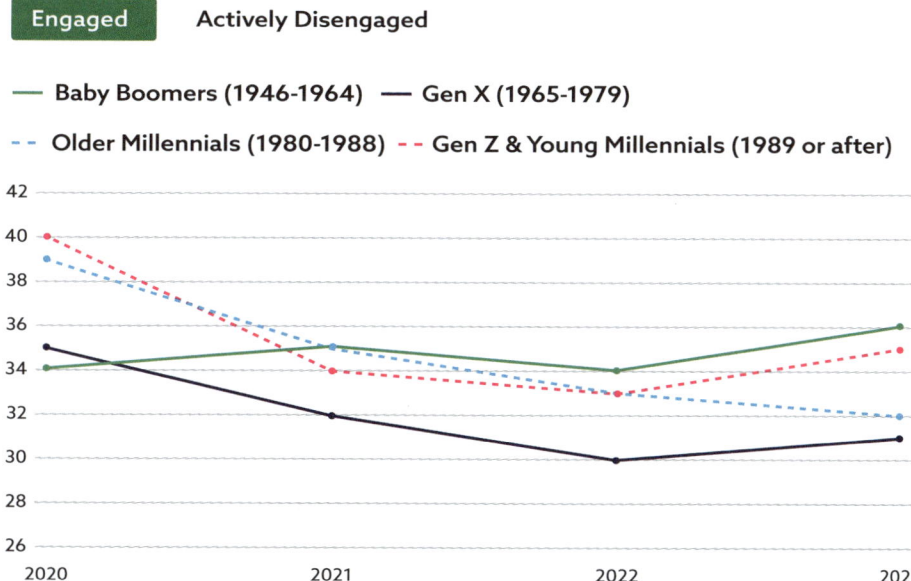

Figure 2: Differences in engagement levels between generations. Younger Workers Feeling Greater Drop in Engagement Than Other Generations.

Millennials and Gen Z employees have seen the greatest decline in feeling cared about by someone at work.

GALLUP RESEARCH 2024

This study confirms my experience as my CARE Principles appeal mostly to Millennials and Generation Z. The problem with this disengaged workforce is that it takes courage and tracking to see it. This research also elucidated my experience with the insurance company. This boss must have been an engaged and privileged baby boomer, leading teams of engaged Baby Boomers. However, this personal example points out the differences between generations on the work floor – differences that demand a tailor-made approach, and depend on more than just adapting yourself to the demands of age groups. Millennials and Gen Z employees have seen the greatest decline in feeling cared about by someone at work, in having opportunities to learn and grow, feeling connected to the mission of the organization, having progress discussions with managers, being given opportunities to develop, and feeling that their opinions count.

Societal changes are happening – whether you are open to seeing them or not – and will influence how you keep your workforce happy, engaged and involved! Let's get further into possible challenges ahead of you if you don't adapt your leadership style to the diverse and multigenerational workforce.

▪ Quiet quitting and other phenomena highly related to stress

Gallup measured a staggering 44% of employees worldwide who say they are stressed. But not all people who feel stressed quit their jobs, start better self-care, or fall out with burnout. Many people continue to work for their non-caring bosses and for non-purposeful organizations. They do not all have the courage to leave and look for a better opportunity for themselves. This phenomenon has been referred to as quiet quitting.[22] If you are new to this term, it refers to: 'Doing the minimum requirements of one's job and putting in no more time, effort, or enthusiasm than absolutely necessary.' 'Quiet quitting' gained significant popularity and widespread media attention in 2022, particularly as it was discussed across various social media platforms, including TikTok, where it became a viral topic. The concept of disengagement however has existed for much longer.

Since Covid, HR professionals and researchers have debated how important this quiet quitting trend is. Recent UK research[23] highlights a gap between the generations in working ethics and engagement. The London School of Economics and Political Science (LSE) conducted research focusing on the UK labour market, identifying significant trends in quiet quitting, especially among younger male workers in the so called 'laptop class'. This study pointed out the shift towards greater work-life balance and the potential implications of reduced working hours on productivity and economic growth. Also in this study, Baby Boomers were the only generation found to continue to work at pre-pandemic levels. Interestingly, this study also revealed that the reason younger generations work fewer hours compared to their elder colleagues was because of unproductive activities like pointless meetings. They are also more open to using artificial intelligence to complete their tasks, making them work fewer hours to obtain the same results. In the agility chapter, we will dive deeper into this phenomenon of not focusing on time spent but on results!

You need all brain in the game!

DEBORAH DUNSIRE, FORMER CEO LUNDBECK

It is interesting to note that this is truly a global phenomenon; in China, tang ping, which translates to 'lying flat', became popular around 2021 as a form of silent protest against the intense work culture, high societal expectations, and the pressures of consumerism. It represents a choice to opt out of the highly competitive rat race, focusing instead on a minimalist lifestyle that rejects the relentless pursuit of work advancements and material success. The 'lying flat' movement is seen as a way for individuals, particularly young people, to push back against the societal norm of overworking and the stress associated with trying to achieve traditional markers of success, such as high-paying jobs, property ownership, and wealth accumulation. Instead, those who embrace 'tang ping' advocate for leading simpler lives with reduced personal and financial burdens, emphasising well-being and personal contentment over societal expectations.

Have you already calculated how many quiet quitters you have? Okay, so now you have quiet quitting, but unfortunately there is worse. Loud quitting is a new trend in which employees openly express negativity about their employer. Like quiet quitting, this phenomenon grew out of The Great Resignation. 'Loud quitting' is a term used to describe a situation where an employee noticeably displays dissatisfaction with their work environment or management as they exit their job, instead of leaving silently or without much fuss. This can involve openly discussing their grievances, whether through social media, with colleagues, or in an exit interview. The aim might be to draw attention to perceived issues within the organization, push for change, or simply vent frustration. This contrasts with 'quiet quitting', where employees disengage from their work without formally resigning, doing only the minimum required and avoiding extra effort.

According to TikTok data, there were over 54 million videos on loud quitting while I was researching it. By the time you read this, that number would certainly have gone up. This trend is gaining so much traction on TikTok that it has been called 'Quit-Tok'. It is quite frightening to watch how people from all over the globe share online calls in which they are made redundant or quit themselves. The damage this does to an organization has never been calculated so far, but it must have a devastating effect on the brand. You might not have noticed it, but another disengagement trend was first spotted on TikTok. 'Bare Minimum Mondays', describing a tendency among employees to do the least work required on Mondays, is a response to workplace pressure and is seen to prioritise well-being over productivity. While this trend is recognised,[24] I couldn't find specific statistics on how widespread the practice is.

Another growing trend is digital nomadism. The number of digital nomads has seen significant growth, particularly following the Covid-19 pandemic, which accelerated remote working trends globally. In the United States alone, the number of digital nomads increased by 131% from 2019, reaching approximately 16.9 million by 2022.[25] The digital nomad population is diverse, spanning various age groups and professions, though it predominantly includes younger individuals who are technically savvy and well educated. Digital nomads tend to work fewer than 40 hours per week on average, and many are taking advantage of geo-arbitrage – living in places where the cost of living is lower than in their home country. This has enabled them to save money and enjoy a flexible lifestyle, though it's worth noting that only a minority continuously travel while working.

The rise in digital nomadism is not without its challenges, however. Issues such as personal safety, loneliness, and managing work and travel logistics are significant concerns for many in this lifestyle. Additionally, the impact on local communities can be profound, with increases in living costs in popular destinations due to higher demands for short-term rentals, which can price out residents. I spend a lot of time in Portugal and the price of real estate has increased substantially since Covid and the increase in digital nomads. Unfortunately, cities like Lisbon became overpriced for my Portuguese friends. As with any trend, some people lose, others win. New concepts like Nomad Stays or Way to Nomad – affordable, nomad-friendly accommodation – have been developed to cater for those travelling while working.

Another trend is 'polywork'.[26] It is not huge in Europe yet, but in the U.S. we see that a growing trend of taking on multiple jobs or roles simultaneously is gaining traction with Generation Z and Millennials. We need to be open-minded about why people take on several jobs. The appeal lies in the flexibility, freedom, and increased income potential it offers. People engage in polywork not just out of financial necessity but also for personal fulfilment, allowing them to explore various interests and skills in parallel. This movement indicates a shift from traditional single-job careers to more fluid and dynamic work lives, driven by personal choice and the changing economic landscape. Another trend we witness is the promadic economy, with more people wanting to continue their job but from another country or plural destinations.

Whether you may or may not have experienced these trends, I hear many stories of demotivated employees who feel no real connection with the organization that pays them. They often stick to their jobs as they feel overwhelmed by the idea of having to look for another job. They are scared that it won't be better at a different job. They don't want to get out of the 'golden cage' as they like their good salaries and perks. Some have completely abandoned the idea of liking the work they do, and simply see it as a harsh reality to earn money, saying, 'It sucks, but hey, the bills need to be paid.' They continue to do whatever is asked of them but prefer to stick to a bare minimum of involvement in their jobs, and find joy, fun, passion, or plain escapism outside the company walls. These people will never feel truly engaged by your organization's goals and ambition and will not fully help you to realise it. They are like a car that never gets out of the third gear; yes, it is moving, but never at its full capacity!

A final trend is not simply something spotted on TikTok, it is a law, adopted by more and more countries. And it started as a movement – 'the right to disconnect' – in France, but has been adopted in more countries. In 2017 it became law. This law aims to forbid companies from requiring employees to engage in work-related communications, like emails, outside of regular work hours. This law stipulates that companies with more than 50 employees must negotiate rules that limit the intrusion of work into employees' private lives, including communications outside of work hours. For companies with fewer than 50 employees, there is a requirement to establish clear guidelines on the right to disconnect. France, Spain, Belgium, Ireland, Italy, Canada, and the Philippines have introduced this law or a similar one over the past years.

These laws and regulations reflect a growing recognition of the need to protect employees from the potential downsides of constant connectivity, especially as work-from-home arrangements become more common. They aim to help employees maintain a healthier work-life balance by clearly delineating work time from personal time. Whether you like it or not, laws, trends, work ethics, and cultural shifts are part of a broader discussion on work-life balance, a shift in demand for more employee autonomy in the wake of pandemic-induced burnouts, and a generational shift in dealing with organizational pressure to be more productive, and how these generations question how important work really is to them. The need for more autonomy, the importance of work-life balance and the idea to work result-based instead of time-clocked monitoring is what today's talent desires.

Should we blame these younger generations? Despite the massive amounts of proof of how a caring leadership style leads to a productive, engaged, and empowered workforce and thus a growing and successful organization, reality shows that most leaders still don't follow this and are not willing to adapt their leadership styles. Why is that? Why don't we have more leaders willing to transform their leadership styles? I guess there are many reasons to be found, but let me share the three main reasons I witness on the work floor.

WHY MANY LEADERS RESIST CHANGE

Many leaders resist change for several reasons, often related to psychological, organizational, and practical factors. Here is my top three witnessed in business.

- **Both leaders and employees hate change.**

A couple of years ago I was asked to reposition a beautiful and well-known family-owned brand. I always start a repositioning exercise with a deep dive into the organization. The internal audit is the first step of a process to understand the people behind the brand. During interviews in this internal audit, it was soon obvious that the CEO, founder, and owner of this company had a very toxic leadership style. As soon as this CEO parked his car, people were warning each other that he had arrived, as most days he entered the building while screaming about everything he saw that was wrong. It could be trash he found in the parking spots, flowers at the reception desk that were old, to a sloppy showroom. The slightest detail could make him explode in anger and verbal abuse.

It didn't stop there. On a daily basis, he treated his staff badly: yelling, criticising, manipulating, lying, playing team members against each other by giving or withholding information to some, and not to others, and micro-managing to the extreme. The worst was probably that he was completely unpredictable: he was sometimes very nice and sweet, giving compliments, but this was soon followed by explosions of rage and violence at a level I had never seen before. All interviews throughout the internal audit indicated that his staff was afraid of him and hardly dared to do anything other than the routine risk-averse tasks. I had never met a workforce on the verge of collective burnout like this one.

When I – in the most cautious way possible – confronted the CEO with my findings, to my surprise, he admitted his bad mood and horrible leadership style. Close to tears, he explained that stress, financial worries, and extreme fatigue had turned him into a horrible manager. I was surprised by his openness when he shared how his company seemed a success story to the outside world, but a constant lack of cash caused him sorrow and stress. With his production unit based in the Far East, the many travels he had to undertake had brought him close to burnout too. Due to his extreme 'command and control' leadership style, he had a weak management team, a bunch of yes-men who were frankly too paralysed to add real value to his firm. They were simply executing his wishes and demands.

During the process of this repositioning job, he had to continue the production follow-up in the Far East and left the Belgian office for weeks. During these weeks, I expected his management team to loosen up and be more relaxed at work, as the big evil boss who caused them trauma was not there. This experience happened long before Zoom calls became the norm, so due to the time difference between Europe and the Far East live contact between them was rare. I could not believe it at first, but what happened when the CEO was abroad was staggering. His management team completely imitated his leadership style and bullied the rest of the staff. Nothing really changed for most of the employees. The bullied people became bullies! I was shocked! I learned later that in psychology this behaviour is often referred to as the 'cycle of abuse'.[27] It reflects the phenomenon where victims of bullying or abuse may in turn exhibit similar abusive behaviours, often to cope with or exert control over their environment. This phenomenon can lead to situations such as sexual or physical abuse on the work floor.

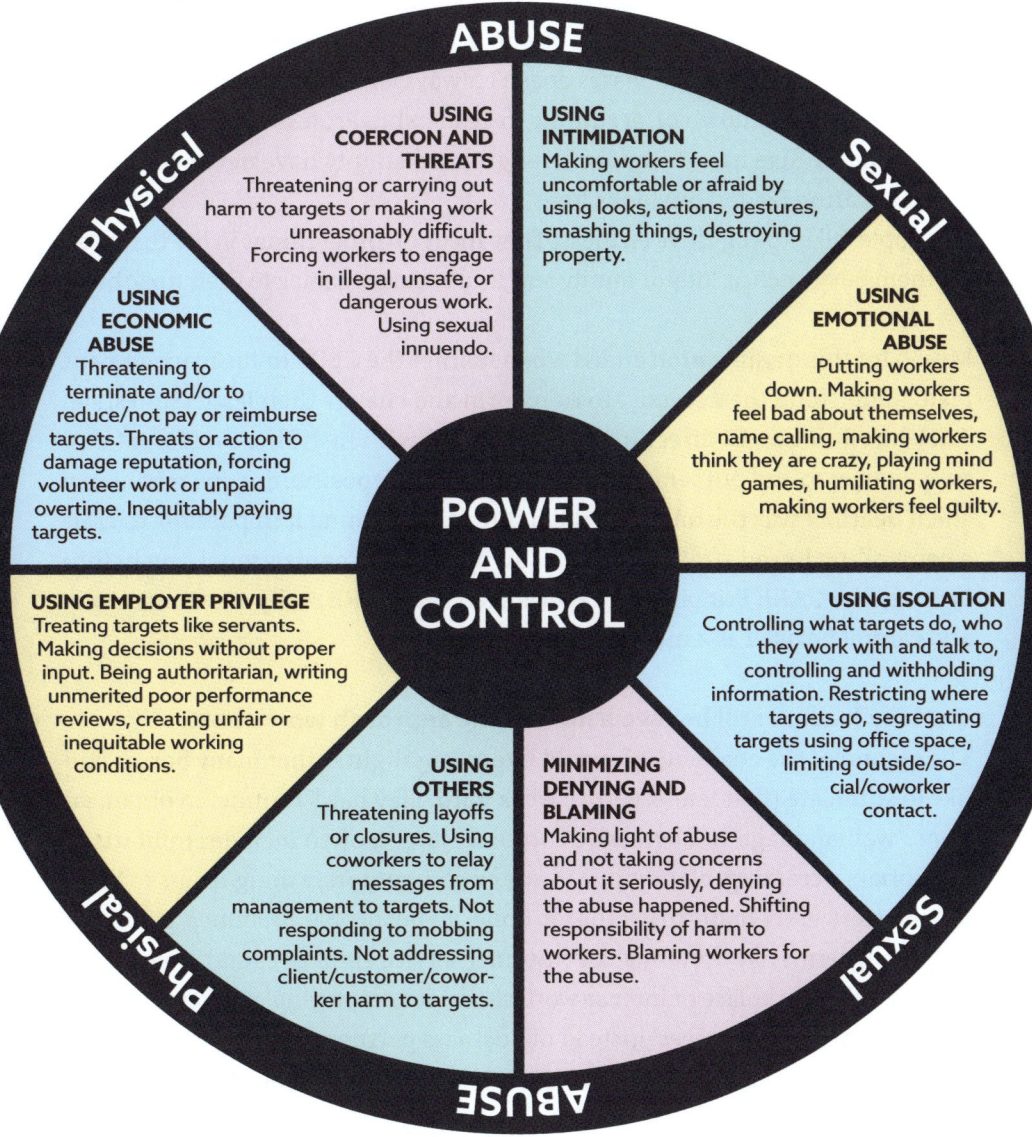

Figure 3: Power and control in the workplace.

The light form of abuse I witnessed in this organization was a very valuable lesson to me. It made me understand that many people prefer to stick to what they know – even if it causes them high levels of stress and anxiety – rather than looking for another job.

This was the most extreme example of toxic leadership I worked with, while realising that more extreme situations do occur. Working for narcissistic, abusive, or other forms of toxic bosses doesn't always lead to people quitting. Many people fear the unknown or, according to Leadership Professor Ronald Riggio:[28]
- People confuse narcissism for strength, and simply have never witnessed what caring leadership looks like.
- People fall into cognitive laziness. They focus on other things in life that keep them busy, such as kids or family and find excuses to stick to their toxic boss.

My job for this organization ended when neither the CEO nor his management team understood the necessity to transform and change their leadership style. They hired a new HR director who was tasked with instilling a different culture. I never found out whether it worked as the repositioning job ended in a silent death. It was the only job I did not finish as I found it impossible to craft a compelling brand strategy for such an uncaring organization. Long before I crafted the CARE Principles, I experienced that CARE really starts internally and cannot be used as a marketing strategy.

■ **Many leaders still believe a militaristic approach works best.**
The second of the challenges I would like to highlight is that many bosses still like to stimulate their teams with a 'work hard, play hard' routine. In organizations, 'war language' or aggressive corporate jargon often includes militaristic metaphors – creating 'war rooms' to attack competitors, asking teams to 'man up' and work extra hours to get the job done, giving people '*dead*lines' to finish a task, using terms like 'frontline' for customer service employees and 'trenches' to reference the workplace or intense work situations, 'capturing' market share and forming 'strategic alliances' instead of business partnerships – as the CEOs believe a militaristic approach and culture is the only way to lead teams to success.

> **What can leaders do today to potentially save the world? Gallup has found one clear answer: Change the way your people are managed.**
>
> JON CLIFTON, CEO GALLUP

You can imagine that this leadership style comes with a boss who pretends to know it all. It is the archetype of the authoritarian boss. This character is typically marked by overbearing confidence, a reluctance to admit lack of knowledge, and a tendency to dismiss the input of others. This archetype shows resistance to collaboration or alternative ideas. We often also see that this type of boss likes to surround himself with a management team of clones, who have grown in their careers focusing on the same skills, communication styles and a go-getter mentality. The kind of 'winners' attitude that says more about the leader than about leadership.

This is the archetype of a successful boss that we have seen over the past couple of decades in movies and in business. Many don't know better. Many fight hard for this type of leader to remain in charge. You just need to look at politics to see how many of these (male) leaders still run the world. Many leaders grew up in this system and fear the unknown. Change introduces uncertainty. Leaders might worry about the outcomes of new strategies or processes, particularly if the current situation is stable and predictable.

I totally understand why a 'command and control' kind of leadership style is successful and still so popular. As a boss, it gives comfort and peace of mind to have a clear top-down approach in decision-making and management. Your decision-making process is centralised and in your own hands. The organizational structure is rigid and clear, and it allows you to set firm guidelines and rules. Job expectations are clear and well defined, leaving no room to freewheel or improvise. For sure in crisis situations where quick and decisive action is needed this leadership style can move mountains, but in general talent demand to give input and want to be seen as a valuable part of the team.

> **If you live your life through the illusion of control, good luck in finding happiness.**
>
> **MO GAWDAT, FORMER CHIEF BUSINESS OFFICER OF GOOGLE X**

■ Egomania rules

Most leaders have huge egos – or at least that appears to be the case. There is significant research on the role of ego in leadership, exploring how personality traits associated with ego, such as narcissism and self-confidence, impact leadership styles and effectiveness. Leadership inherently involves a degree of power and control over others. This can inflate the ego as leaders may begin to feel uniquely capable or indispensable. The power can also create a self-reinforcing loop where success leads to more confidence, which can slip into overconfidence or arrogance. Being in the spotlight and visibility can feed the ego, as human nature often equates attention with value or superiority.

In search of new leaders, recruitment agencies, headhunters and executive search have created assessments that often still focus on leadership traits like confidence, assertiveness, and decisiveness. There is nothing wrong with these traits, but they can lead to egotistical behaviour, sometimes at the expense of equally and important leadership qualities like empathy and humility. The biggest issue we witness is that many leaders face loneliness and isolation in their job. They have worries and issues they rarely can share with anyone. Without sufficient checks and balances, without mentors or trusted and honest advisors around them, leaders may lack the feedback needed to keep their ego in check. The isolation can also lead to a disconnect from the team, enhancing an 'us versus them' mindset.

Ego-driven leaders are often more transactional in their approach, focusing on exchanges of rewards for performance and maintaining control. In contrast, transformational leaders, who are generally less ego driven, inspire and motivate employees through vision and personal connections, which often leads to higher levels of employee satisfaction and productivity. In competitive environments, leaders might feel the need to assert their ego to protect their position or influence within the organization. A friend of mine had a top position as the number 3 in a global company. Between her and the global CEO was one person. This person's only occupation was to hold on to his chair and position. His concern was no longer the business's challenges and issues; his daily concern and actions were all about keeping his seat right under the CEO. She got fed up of this power and ego game and resigned.

Self-knowledge and self-awareness are great and important traits of leaders, but when your ego gets in the way of your functioning as a leader, it can jeopardise your organization. As with many things in life, it is a balancing act. Balancing ego is crucial in leadership. Effective leaders manage their ego, ensuring it does not overpower their ability to lead wisely and empathetically. They leverage their self-confidence for decision-making and motivating others while remaining open to feedback and other perspectives. They understand they do not have all the wisdom; they dare to show vulnerability and say they don't have all knowledge and answers.

Finally, studies on emotional intelligence (EQ) have shown that leaders with high EQ tend to be less driven by ego. They are more aware of their own emotions and those of others, enabling them to manage relationships more effectively and foster a positive work environment. In a world where machines are taking over knowledge and are becoming better at it than the human IQ, it is time to embrace EQ and understand the power of letting go of the egomaniac approach of leadership and embrace a more eco-minded togetherness with the team. The CARE Principles leadership is about connecting through your heart with others, and not solely through your head. It takes effort, deep insights, a lot of introspection and vulnerability to dare to lead from the heart. It is not what we have learned from most of our predecessors. But it is what is needed in these transformational times.

> **We don't live in an era of change; we live in a change of era.**
>
> **PROFESSOR ROTMANS**

Remember, evolution is the only thing that keeps the world going and change is coming. Many younger and more diverse generations don't want to work for – or are not fully engaged with – the above types of leaders.

Think about the fact that our future life will no longer be divided into four very different life-phases:
- Childhood & play
- Young life & education
- Parents & work
- Elderly & pension

From now on, we will all be cycling through work, upskilling, resting moments, learning curves, and play stages several times throughout our careers and lifespan. We can better embrace it and make it fun and playful, right?

Finally, I do want to add that I know many caring organizations who try to offer more flexibility to their employees but face outdated legislation and huge bureaucratic regulations. Government laws often run behind and this does not help organizations who want to innovate in their human resources strategies. What are you waiting for? Jump in and grow the contemporary leadership skills demanded by your team! But be gentle and compassionate to yourself and your team. Change is not so easy, and you will have to overcome many obstacles.

I have only visited Japan once – and I loved it – but working for the Japanese company Fujifilm has made me aware of some great insights they use in their lives. One of these insights is called Kaizen. You can apply Kaizen to your personal and professional life. Kaizen is a Japanese term meaning 'change for the better' or 'continuous improvement'. It is a philosophy that focuses on continuous improvement. The concept of Kaizen involves making small, incremental changes regularly to improve efficiency and quality. It emphasises productivity but also has an eye for the human aspects such as improving work life and fostering a team-oriented culture that values contribution from every member. Throughout this book, you will find more examples of Japanese wisdom as extra inspiration!

PODCAST INTERVIEW

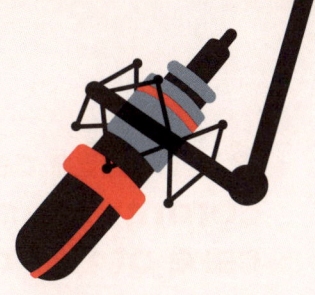

WITH BART VAN OLPHEN, CEO AND FOUNDER OF FISH TALES

If Japanese wisdom is not your cup of tea, get inspired by listening to Bart Van Olphen, chief, and founder of the Dutch company Fish Tales,[29] a company with a mission and clear purpose that is conquering the world! Bart van Olphen is a pioneering entrepreneur and sustainability advocate, renowned as the founder and CEO of Fish Tales, a company dedicated to providing sustainably sourced seafood. With a deep passion for the ocean and a commitment to environmental stewardship, Bart has become a leading voice in the sustainable fishing movement. Under his leadership, Fish Tales has revolutionised the seafood industry by partnering with small-scale fisheries around the world, ensuring that their practices are environmentally friendly and socially responsible.

Bart's innovative approach not only promotes the health of our oceans but also supports the livelihoods of fishing communities, making Fish Tales a beacon of sustainability and ethical business practices in the global market. His vision and dedication have earned him recognition and accolades, solidifying his status as a transformative figure in the quest for a more sustainable and equitable food system. Bart is an unconventional leader who is fighting against very conservative powers of a traditional fishing industry that is not willing to show much change. Fighting the old and conservative powers can be draining, but that never kept Bart from continuing his quest and fight for a more equal world in the fishing industry. Bart is one of the most passionate entrepreneurs I have met in my podcast interviews! This interview is a beautiful proof that if you work from a clear purpose and you have the guts to change the system, you will be successful.

If we take care of the fishing communities, they will take care of the oceans.

BART VAN OLPHEN, FOUNDER FISH TALES

Bart's tips are:
- The power is with the consumers; they are the driver of change within society.
- The power is with the younger generation of consumers today. They will determine what all industries need to do.
- If businesses don't listen to the consumers, they won't exist anymore.

https://spotifyanchor-web.app.link/e/JwHHNFwtgMb

PLAY SECTION 4

THE MULTIGENERATIONAL WORKFORCE IS TODAY'S REALITY

Figure 4: Generational categories.

WHAT IS A MULTIGENERATIONAL WORKFORCE?

The work floor is seeing a phenomenon that has never occurred before. There are now up to 5 different generations working together. All these generations working simultaneously is a first in modern history. It is quite logical that the challenges this brings are new to current leaders. In this chapter, we will concentrate on the four generations most often spotted working together today. We will deliberately avoid talking about the silent generation here, as well as Generation Alpha for the simple reason that the first generation is in its nineties, and the youngest are teenagers. Both are rarely seen in companies. Why are so many different generations together on the work floor? It is down to a combination of demographic, economic and social factors. Here are the three most common:

- **Increased life expectancy, better health, and later retirement:** Advances in healthcare and overall well-being have enabled people to live longer, healthier lives, encouraging older generations to remain in the workforce longer than in the past. Combine this with economic factors, concerns about inadequate pensions and lifelong learning and you see more elderly people continuing to work. They have the experience and knowledge younger managers often lack.

- **Technological requirements:** It started with a need for digitally skilled and thus younger generations. Due to today's fast growth of technologies such as AI we see younger people in management positions. They have knowledge and skills the older generations simply don't have.

- **Diversity and inclusion efforts:** Many organizations still struggle to gain and retain talent from a different background, because many organizations remain 'white' environments. Embracing gender and age diversity in leadership positions is one way to work on DEI goals and objectives. More on this topic in the agility chapter!

A multigenerational workforce is one in which the employees span different generations. To refresh your marketing lessons, let's have a look at the four generations found on the work floor today and the characteristics of each generation.

The 4 generations working together and their different leadership needs
Before we dive deeper into each generation, it is interesting to understand why each generation has different expectations from life and thus from leadership. The American authors William Strauss and Neil Howe[30] analysed decennia of history in their book *'The Fourth Turning'*. They defined how modern history moves in cycles, each one lasting about the length of a long human life, about 80 years. Within each cycle of 80 years, four 20-year eras – or 'turnings' – can be spotted. Their theory illuminates the past, explains the present, and reimagines the future and explains how each generation reacts differently to these 'turnings'. Their model is based on American history, and I don't want to go into it too deeply, but there is some correlation to be found in their thinking and the behaviour of generations.

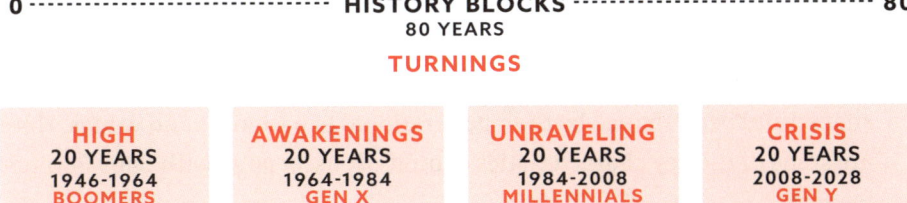

Figure 5: The four periods of generations.

The four turnings or periods that define history according to the Strauss-Howe generational theory are:
1. **The high:** A period of cohesive societal rebuilding and strengthening after a crisis. Institutions are strong, and individualism is weak.
2. **The awakening:** A time of spiritual revival and rebellion against established institutions. Society focuses on the development of personal and spiritual autonomy, often at the expense of civic order.
3. **The unraveling:** A time when institutions are distrusted, and individualism is strong and flourishing. The fabric of society thins leading to a fraying of social order.
4. **The crisis:** This is a turning point where society faces a major crisis. It culminates with the rebuilding of institutions and the commencing of a new cycle with a high.

This theory becomes interesting when you plot it onto our recent history and generations.

1. **The high & Baby Boomers:** As mentioned, 'the high' is a period of cohesive societal rebuilding and strengthening after a crisis, like in the post-war period of 1946 till 1964. The generation of Baby Boomers were born in this period. This generation are typically idealistic, passionate, and look to solve the world's deeper problems.

They have had a significant impact on leadership styles and workplace dynamics. As they have held leadership positions for several decades now, Baby Boomers have developed distinct leadership traits that have both shaped and been shaped by their generational experiences and values. Here are some of the key characteristics commonly associated with Baby Boomer leaders:

- **They value hard work and dedication:** Baby Boomers are often characterised by their strong work ethic. They typically value long hours and high commitment to their jobs, which can be attributed to the economic prosperity and job security that marked their formative years.
- **Their leadership style is hierarchical and command-control:** Baby Boomer leaders tend to prefer a more traditional top-down approach to management. They often believe in a structured hierarchy and clear distinctions between roles and responsibilities within an organization.
- **Loyalty matters to them:** While they may employ a hierarchical style, many Baby Boomers also place a high value on personal relationships and loyalty within the workplace. They tend to be more formal in their communication but emphasise building strong professional relationships.
- **They are consensus seekers:** They often strive for consensus and are typically diplomatic in their approach to leadership. They prefer to make decisions that incorporate the inputs and agreement of others, reflecting a balance between individual action and collective harmony.
- **Financial security and stability are key:** Having experienced economic prosperity, this post-war generation often emphasise financial success and stability in their professional endeavours. This focus translates into leadership that prioritises organizational growth and financial health.
- **Competitive and change resistant:** They often thrive on challenges and competition in the business environment. While this is not universal, some Baby Boomer leaders can be resistant to change, especially regarding new technologies and shifts in traditional business models. However, many have also adapted and embraced change as necessary over time, but it doesn't come naturally to most.

- **Mentorship and development:** These leaders often value mentorship and take a keen interest in developing younger employees. They tend to be generous with their time in coaching and guiding the next generations.

In family-owned businesses this generation is still spotted and often called the 'pater familias', still pulling the strings. Specifically in family-owned businesses they often still dictate the culture and management style. They are mainly male, as in that generation not many women were allowed to lead companies. In the case that these Baby Boomers pass on the family business to their kids, it is painful to sometimes hear amazing female leaders who talk about how their dads still treat them more poorly compared to their brothers who are also part of the management. But this generation deserves respect as it is the post-war generation who have built thriving organizations.

2. **The awakening and Generation X:** If we continue to follow the turnings in modern history, this period is about 1964–1984 and links to Gen X, born between 1965 and 1980. This 'awakening' turning can be seen as a time of spiritual revival and rebellion against established institutions. Growing up in the eighties, this generation witnessed the Cold War, nuclear threats, IRA bombings, and more, which made them aware that peace is not a given. But under influence of their parents, most of them choose a path of hard work and discipline. Being a first generation of couples both working full-time, they started to pay attention to work-life balance.
They can be found in most management positions at present and are often a blend of traditional and contemporary approaches. My generation is probably the first one in which women work fulltime in organizations. Female leaders of this group have mostly learned from the male bosses how to become pragmatic and result-oriented leaders. To break the glass ceiling, women had to develop their male traits. Some of these female leaders have lost touch with their softer, female side as they had to 'man up' and fight for their spots at the board level. However, most of this generation has learned from their Millennial employees and are effective leaders in managing diverse and dynamic teams.

Gen X leaders bring a blend of pragmatism, autonomy, and adaptability to their management styles. We are also referred to as the repair generation, stuck between post-war parents who tell us to be brave and work hard, and our children who blame us for having screwed up their world. We try to repair, to fix things and to clean up the debris. Cleaning, fixing, and repairing is our calling. Their most common leadership traits are:

- **Autonomous and independent focus:** Gen Xers are known for valuing independence and self-sufficiency in the workplace. This stems partly from growing up during a time of changing societal structures and economic uncertainty. As leaders, they tend to encourage autonomy and empower their team members to work independently.
- **Tech-oriented:** We were still young enough when personal computers, the internet and mobile phones arrived, so we are generally comfortable with technology and often integrate digital solutions into our business practices.
- **Results-driven:** Generation X places a strong emphasis on results and efficiency. They are known for a pragmatic approach to leadership, focusing on what works best rather than sticking to traditional methods or hierarchical structures.
- **Adaptable and flexible:** This generation has experienced significant economic and social flux, which has fostered a capacity for adaptability. In leadership, this translates into a willingness to pivot strategies, embrace new ideas, and adjust to changing business environments.
- **Work-life balance:** Gen X leaders are pivotal in shifting workplace culture towards greater work-life balance. They value the importance of time spent outside of work, both for themselves and their employees. This approach to leadership often leads to more flexible working conditions within their organizations.
- **Direct and clear communication:** Generation X is known for valuing straightforward, clear communication. They tend to cut through rhetoric and focus on substance, which is reflected in their communication as leaders.
- **Questioning authority:** Growing up during times when distrust in government and corporations was increasing, Gen Xers often carry a healthy scepticism of authority. As leaders, they dare to question the status quo and encourage their teams to do the same, fostering an en-

vironment where debate and dissent are welcomed as part of the decision-making process. However, they are professionally mentored by the Baby Boomers and often question authority in unofficial gatherings.
- **Professional development is key to them:** As Gen X witnessed the technological revolution, they understand the value of continuous learning, so Gen X leaders often prioritise the development of their team members. They support career development and continuous education, understanding that these are key to long-term organizational success.

3. **The unraveling and the role of Millennials:** Between 1984 and 2008 the turning is called 'the unraveling'. A time when institutions are distrusted, and individualism is strong and flourishing. This connects to Generation Y, better known as Millennials, born between 1980 and 1994. This generation was the first to give leaders grey hair as they started to demand another leadership style. This was the first generation to really prioritise good work-life balance. They tend to favour flat organizational structures and like teamwork. They are probably also the first generation that was open about mental issues, stress problems and their search for purpose in life. They clearly started the demand for new leadership skills! Their leadership style is often influenced by the technological and economic environments they grew up in, as well as their educational background and social values. They will continue to crack down on the linear approach towards work and career. They will push the habit of combining focus periods in which they work hard, followed by extended breaks for various reasons. Recreation, upskilling, or any other pursuit that they find necessary to keep their mental health in balance will be more important to them than the linear career. Google understood this and has integrated this thinking into their daily business. In a podcast interview[31] with Thierry Geerts, the ex-CEO of Google, he confirmed that whenever you do a job that demands real focus, they are allowed to take the same amount of time to disconnect. This openness to let people work at their own pace, time and place of choice is an attitude that is not yet widespread. Still, it can make you wonder why Google allows this... isn't this the best way to get the most out of your people? Let them thrive, remain engaged and perform at their best? I challenge you to think about this and how you could install such a habit in your organization!

Other leadership traits of the Millennial generation are:
- **Tech-forward:** Millennials are the first generation to grow up with the internet and digital technology as a central part of their lives, which makes them highly adept at leveraging technology in the workplace. They are comfortable with digital communication tools, data analytics, and remote working technologies.
- **Collaborative mindset:** Millennials tend to favour a collaborative and inclusive approach to leadership. They are more likely to seek input and feedback from their team and encourage a participative decision-making process. This approach often leads to a more democratic and less hierarchical workplace culture.
- **Value-driven:** They are known for their desire to work for companies and causes that align with their personal values. As leaders, they often emphasise corporate social responsibility, sustainability, and ethical practices. They seek to make an impact that extends beyond financial success.
- **Flexibility rules:** Like Generation X, Millennials place a strong emphasis on achieving a healthy work-life balance. They are more likely to support flexible working hours, remote work options, and a results-oriented work environment that allows employees to manage their own time effectively.
- **Feedback-oriented:** Millennial leaders often thrive on feedback, both giving and receiving it. They typically implement regular and structured feedback mechanisms to foster personal and professional growth within their teams.
- **Mentoring and lifelong learning:** They view continuous learning as crucial and are committed to personal and professional development. As leaders, they tend to be supportive mentors who are invested in nurturing the growth of their team members through training programmes, workshops, and continuous learning opportunities.
- **Innovation-driven:** Having witnessed rapid technological and social changes, Millennial leaders are often oriented towards innovation. They are open to experimenting with new ideas, disrupting traditional business models, and adapting to changing market dynamics.

- **Empathetic:** Millennials often bring a high level of empathy to their leadership style. They strive to understand and address the individual needs of their team members, which can lead to a more supportive and cohesive working environment.

4. **The crisis and Generation Z:** If the turnings model is correct, the current crisis we face started around 2008 with the financial crisis and will end around 2028. The 'crisis' turning is literally a turning point where society faces a major crisis. It culminates with the rebuilding of institutions and the commencing of a new cycle with a high. In this period, my generation had kids: Gen Z, born between the late nineties till 2012 approximately.

Some people from generation Z are still studying. The oldest have gradually started to work and due to their digital and technological skills, will probably end up in leadership positions at a young age. They are digital natives, and devices are a natural part of their lives. We often joke that our daughters' phones have grown into their hands; you rarely see them without them.

It is probably too early to tell as their numbers on the work floor are still growing, but we can assume this generation will demand flexibility, mentorship, personal growth, and the need to contribute to a purposeful and positive organizational culture. Influenced by a world struggling with pandemics, terrorism, mass shootings in the US, and climate change, Gen Z probably prizes stability, meaningful work, social advocacy, and protecting their mental health. Taking frequent career shifts for diverse reasons had already started with the Millennials, and for sure Generation Z will not expect to stay in the same organization for the long run, unless they are truly convinced and incentivised. Careers are just one aspect of their 'liquid' lifestyles in which they do not want to be defined by nationality, class, gender, personal interests, etc. They see themselves, always in transition to the next phase. They are committed to contributing. Making a positive impact and contribution to change and a way forward out of the crisis is what drives them.

If you want to appeal to this generation, having a purpose will help you to inspire them as they are looking for a job that is a manifestation of their personal set of values. So, start to think about fast and fun onboarding processes, fast-track options for career moves, personal and professional development, and training tools as this will all be necessary to entertain and keep this generation on board, alert and fully engaged. Fast is a word that is important to them as they are easily bored. This generation suffers quickly from a bore out: a state of dissatisfaction and demotivation because they feel bored and unchallenged at work.

In many countries, the official retirement age is being pushed back to cope with ageing populations and the financial strains on pension systems. This trend might suggest that Generation Z could have to work longer than previous generations before they can fully retire. Combine this trend with changing work patterns and you understand why for this generation the boundaries between professional life and private life will continue to blur. They will wear in the office what they wear for leisure, they will watch Netflix on the company's laptop, they will complete personal tasks at work and work tasks at home, and they will probably gossip in meetings with colleagues like they would with friends. In short, work and life are fully integrated, interconnected and a complete mash-up for this generation.

Here is what we further predict for their leadership needs:
- **Digital natives:** Even more so than Millennials, Gen Z has been immersed in technology from a very young age. They are extremely comfortable with the digital world, which includes a proficiency in multitasking across multiple platforms and devices. In leadership, they are likely to leverage advanced technology and digital tools to enhance productivity and engagement. They are going to school in an era of artificial intelligence, and school had to adapt overnight to work done by ChatGPT. They are quick to see the advantages and like cutting corners if that means less hard work has to be put in and technology can do it for you.
- **Independence is crucial:** While they value collaboration, many Gen Z individuals also appreciate autonomous working conditions. They might demand a leadership style that trusts them to complete their tasks without constant oversight, preferring a more hands-off management approach.
- **Desire for transparency and authenticity:** Honesty and integrity are highly valued by Gen Z. They tend to seek leaders who are transparent about business practices and who are authentic in their communications. Any perceived hypocrisy or inauthenticity can be particularly off-putting to

this generation. They are internet savvy and can find the truth about anyone in a couple of clicks. Their love of a leader can turn into hate overnight.

- **Diversity, Equity and Inclusion:** Inclusivity and diversity come naturally to them. Growing up among other kids of all colours, backgrounds, religions, genders, and neurodiversity while spending most of their days online, they have less bias compared to the older generations when it comes to DEI. They expect leaders to not only talk about these values but also to actively implement policies that enhance diversity and inclusion. This generation will find it very strange to work in all-white company, while their school friends are a mix of everything that society offers.
- **No patience:** Gen Z workers tend to be ambitious and look for opportunities to advance quickly within their organizations. They may seek out leaders who provide clear pathways for career growth and who are invested in their professional development. They have little patience for learning the skills and waiting in line to climb the career ladder. They also prefer direct communication tools like SMS or WhatsApp to mail.
- **Mental health and well-being come first:** This generation places a high premium on mental health and overall well-being. Leadership styles that prioritise work-life balance, mental health days, and support for personal well-being will likely be important to Gen Z. They are also the first generation to talk openly about this, helping the stigma around it to disappear.
- **Social and environmental responsibility:** They are particularly concerned with social and environmental issues. They respect and follow leaders who not only address these issues but also incorporate sustainable practices into their business models. Of course they do not always live according to their values, so they do shop online and order a $5 T-shirt at the Chinese e-commerce site SHEIN. Their behaviour is often described as irrational and contradictory by older generations.
- **Resilience:** Having grown up during global crises such as the Covid-19 pandemic, Gen Z values adaptability and resilience not only in themselves but also in their leaders. They appreciate leadership that can navigate through uncertainty and change. However, it is also a generation that grew up with both parents working, and who often praised them for nothing. Afraid of exclusion, this generation grew up with medals for finishing a game, instead of winning it. They grew up without the benefits of boredom and the hard reality of life might still hit them if they have bosses who are not as indulgent as their parents.

As Gen Z continues to mature and move into more significant roles in the workplace, their values and experiences will inevitably shape their approach to leadership and influence organizational cultures. Their expectations for rapid technological integration, social responsibility, and inclusive practices will likely set new standards in leadership paradigms. Their AI skills will bring them faster into board meetings and management committees. You had better prepare for them because you will need this generation if you want to grow your business significantly!

The future of work is full of complex challenges, and they won't be solved by one generation of leaders or decision-makers.

KIRA COPPERMAN, EXECUTIVE COACH AND AUTHOR

Without wanting to fall into clichéd thinking and paying too much attention to the 'turnings', there is some truth to generational psychology. Each generation is marked or at least under the influence of the world events, trends, moral values, and, of course, economic conditions in which they grow up. It influences their thinking, behaviour, and expectations. Today's leaders need to get everyone involved, engaged, connected and performant. Throw into the generational cocktail other ingredients of diversity such as gender, ethnicity, sexual orientation, racial background, religion, neurodiversity, and disability and you understand that the task is challenging. All generations, but specifically Millennials and Gen Z want to feel they belong, and that they are respected, independently of age, race, or gender.

The brightest talents – of all ages and backgrounds – will leave the organization if they feel that they are not heard, and not respected; if they feel there is no sense of belonging; if they feel your culture does not prioritise collaboration; if they sense that people cannot bring their whole authentic selves to work. This leads to phenomena such as identity covering,[32] meaning that individuals downplay or hide certain aspects of their identity to conform to societal or organizational norms. Again, think of ethnicity, gender, sexual orientation, religion, or other characteristics to avoid potential bias, discrimination, or discomfort in each context.

One of the pitfalls we face is that we are attracted to sameness. It is so comfortable to surround yourself with people of the same age, social background, and similar education. You watch the same series, drink the same coffee and often your kids go to the same schools. We will need to dare to leave this comfort zone, as you need younger and diverse talent. No doubt about that. We need to look at the challenges as opportunities. We need to stop focusing on the differences between generations, but on what connects them: talent, drive, and additional skillsets. Together you are stronger and more prepared for the future. Through collaboration you can create a culture of mutual respect, a safe space in which people want to learn from each other across ages and career stages.

I would like to end this chapter with an extraordinary leader: Ali E. Cevik. Ali had crafted an employee manifesto together with his team that I discovered by chance on LinkedIn. I reached out to him, and he immediately agreed to a podcast interview that you'll find below. We have kept in touch since then, as he remains a leader I admire deeply for his unconventional, caring and truly trusting leadership skills. Check out the podcast episode below by simply scanning the QR code.

PODCAST INTERVIEW

WITH ALI E. CEVIK, FOUNDER AND CEO HR-ON.

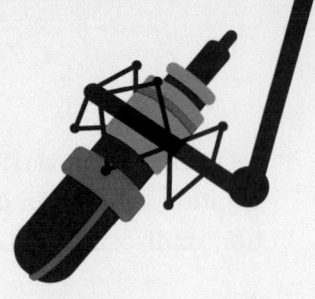

Ali E. Cevik is the founder and CEO of HR-ON[33], a Danish software company that specialises in providing end-to-end cloud-based solutions for recruitment and staff management. Born into a rural, agricultural Turkish community, he started his journey as a shepherd, a role that introduced him to teamwork and responsibility from a young age. His family later moved to Denmark, where he embarked on a new chapter, adapting to a new culture and education system. Cevik pursued higher education in Denmark, graduating with a master's degree in Russian language and economics. His career took a significant turn when he began working as an international adviser to prestigious organizations like the UN, the EU, and the World Bank. He also worked as a career coach, assisting professionals in enhancing their careers with international jobs. In 2012, leveraging his extensive experience in HR and organizational development, Cevik founded HR-ON. The company has since earned recognition for its innovative HR solutions, receiving three Børsen Gazelle awards, the EY Entrepreneur of the Year Award, and forming an official partnership with LinkedIn. Ali is a regular guest on Danish TV and on stages to share his vision of what future leadership looks like.

My people can take as many paid holidays as they want, and work when and from where they want.

ALI E. CEVIK, FOUNDER HR-ON

Ali's journey from shepherd to CEO is a testament to the transformative power of ambition, education, vision, leadership, and hard work. His story inspires many within and outside the HR industry, illustrating how diverse experiences and backgrounds can contribute to success in the contemporary business world!

https://spotifyanchor-web.app.link/e/QNk73DwtgMb

Can't wait to read about COLLABORATION?

PLAY SECTION 5

COLLABORATION IS FUNDAMENTAL

Collaboration and partnerships will be key for a future-proof company. You may already have realised that dealing with the complex challenges we face means that you'll need to reach out to others to win the battle together. As strange as it may seem, reaching out to others starts inside your company, as you will need to break down silos to outperform your competitors. Why? Outperforming your competitors today is one thing but preparing your company to be an attractive employer to the next generation is another. But there is another paradigm shift that might happen to leadership and that needs you to be open about collaborating with others. With greater democratisation efforts comes more decentralised decision-making and the need for a collective and collaborative mindset.

This collaborative mindset is not only necessary for team members, but it will also apply to leaders. Leadership has always been about a single person who controls in a top-down approach others. In the future this might alter, and leadership will become an activity that is shared and distributed among several members of the organization. This means we need to be open to adapt the mindset, work processes, rewards and thinking of leadership. To make sure you are ready to share your leadership responsibilities, empower small teams, shift decision-making and speed up the learning abilities of your staff, check the hurdles list below because if your organization is not structured differently, it might not work.

POSSIBLE COLLABORATION HURDLES

- **Culture issues:** In some companies, office workers feel superior to factory workers and refuse to collaborate to resolve issues that could help level up productivity. This attitude is frequently spotted at companies where the management has little respect for anybody below them. This kind of toxic internal culture might seem like a relic from the past, but unfortunately it is still around.
- **Pointless meeting culture:** I continue to be surprised at how pointless meetings have become the norm again in a post-Covid world! Meetings in which no real decisions are taken. Meetings in which the bosses who are responsible for decisions are not present, so basically meetings that keep the people from their real job.
- **Island mentality:** There are often huge visible and invisible walls between departments. Department managers focus on delivering maximum revenue and profit, often at the expense of other departments. That seems illogical, but it is the reality in most companies, as managers often get opposing KPIs.[34] Under such a regime, it's little wonder that the urge to collaborate is quite low, as people are punished financially for doing so.
- **Hierarchical structures:** This can make the organization slow and unprepared to adapt to the demands of the market. In this type of structure, younger employees in more junior positions often go unheard. With the technological issues facing most companies today, however, it might help to pull in these younger profiles in a more horizontal chain of command.
- **Bureaucracy:** Transparency is often lacking due to internal bureaucracy. Having too many levels of management can obstruct internal communication and impede fast decision-making. Finally, in structures like this, power and responsibility are reserved for management levels throughout the organization, leaving little or no empowerment for the rest of the staff.

With business's role in society being redefined and a new generation demanding a different approach to work, a deeper level of care is called for. And with automation, robotisation and deep machine learning on our doorstep, we'll need to rethink workforce structure and working experience once and for all. This reinvention can be accomplished on different levels depending on your organization's readiness, size, goals, skills, and market needs. But if you are convinced that your company should do a major rethink, be sure to include technology and to create something bold enough to meet societal changes. Lifelong learning, agile skills training, moving faster and adapting to a far more diverse workforce and world will be part of your company's future challenges.

In my first book, I wrote a compelling case of how a different organizational structure and a better internal collaboration created a huge advantage for the university hospital of Brussels during Covid. Later I had the honour of interviewing Marc Noppen, the CEO of the Brussels University Hospital. Check out this wise man's interview here![35] When you are done listening to Marc, have a look at how poorly organizations collaborate – a staggering truth I discovered through collaboration with Ivox, a purpose-driven market research agency.

CARE SCAN TOOL: DISCOVER YOUR ORGANIZATIONAL FLAWS AND WHERE TO START CARE

Towards the end process of writing my first book: *'Does your brand CARE? Building a better world with the CARE Principles'*, I got in touch with Ivox[36], a market research agency with an impact-focused CEO: Hans Verhoeven. I explained to Hans and his team what the CARE framework was all about and asked if they could help me develop a methodology to test how organizations scored on it. Enter the CARE Scan, a baseline measurement inquiry tool that exists today in two formats. The employee CARE Scan tests how caring your organization is in the eyes of your employees. The second variant is aimed at business-to-business customers and demonstrates what your business clients think of you.

Hans and his teams have done two Belgian employee benchmark studies since the launch of the CARE Scan[37], indicating the overall tendency of CARE in Belgium. The overall Belgian CARE score is 58%, and it might not come as a surprise that collaboration scores the lowest of all four Principles: only 53%.

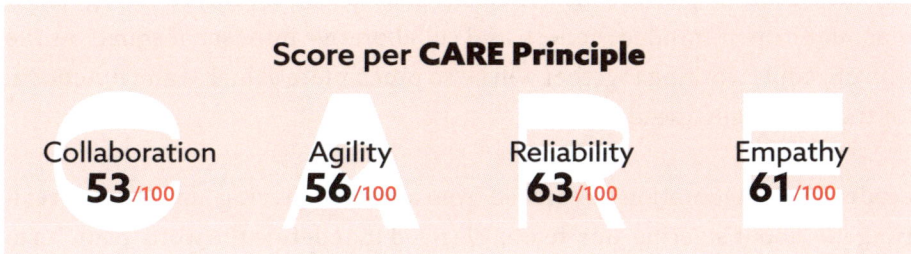

Figure 6: Care Scan score per CARE Principle.

Internal collaboration scores in the benchmark study reveal a 54% score, but after having done several CARE Scans within organizations, I saw that the reality is that quite often the internal collaboration results scored even lower than the benchmark study reveals. Collaboration with clients, stakeholders and green efforts for the planet results are not great either.

Figure 7: Care Scan collaboration scores.

On all levels collaboration is an issue, and it is a key fundamental component scientifically proven to be linked to intuition, trust, purpose, energy, and communication. If you are curious to find out how well your organization scores on the CARE Scan, reach out to Ivox.be and they will be more than happy to set up this baseline inquiry for your company!

Collaboration is about writing a new social contract with each other. It is no longer about steering a team in a one-way, order-giving sense. It is no longer about command and control. It is not about holding back information to others as a tool of power, nor is it about acting as a 'know-it all' kind of boss. Collaboration is about involving all needed individuals to achieve your goals. It is about an open-minded, honest, and collaborative mindset of equals, as the sum of people working together will be so much more valuable and functional for the challenges ahead of you.

Leadership collaboration has moved from a belief of having 'my' team, to realising it is about steering 'our' team. We need to redefine the word 'team' as to realise the goals, ambitions, and dreams of your organization, you will need a network of people: people who report to you directly, people who do not report to you directly, and people outside of your organization who are nowhere in the organigram of your organization, but who are crucial to the success of your plans. Successful collaboration is about a mind shift in understanding that is it no longer about your ego-driven decisions, but about eco-system thinking and acting. Forget the 'I-thinking' and start to replace it with 'WE-thinking'.

So, let's dive into the five necessary steps to adapt your leadership style for a more productive and better collaboration. If you follow this step-by-step approach, I can assure you that your teams will work better together. If you believe you have no use for all five steps, skip the one that you have no trouble with and move over to the next one. But do understand that it is similar to building blocks: you need a strong foundation of trust to create productive and efficient collaboration. And to build that trust and psychological safety, you will need both your brain power and your gut feeling! Surprisingly, the number one issue, crucial for collaborative success, is intuition. Let's better understand why it is crucial to listen to your gut and instinct. Let's talk about the power of intuition.

THE 5 STEPS OF SUCCESSFUL COLLABORATION

STEP 1: INTUITION

What does collaboration have to do with intuition, I hear you wonder? Intuition refers to the ability to understand or know something immediately, based on feelings rather than facts or analysis. It is often described as a 'gut feeling' or an instinctive response that leaders can experience when making decisions. Intuition can be seen as a form of 'unconscious intelligence' and is necessary alongside analytical thinking for making well-rounded decisions. It is something we all have, but we also quite often ignore it. For many leaders, it is seen as the opposite of reason. It is also often seen as soft and useless in the hard binary world of business, knowledge, and data-driven decisions.

Do you really need to trust your gut feeling to get to a productive and successful collaboration?

Definitely! To have a successful collaboration, intuition is a founding step as unconsciously it helps us to define if we truly trust our colleagues or bosses, or not. Intuition helps us to open to others and show vulnerability, an important aspect of trust. We tell ourselves that we are rational beings and that we make all decisions based on clear data and rational analytical processes. Think again and dare to question that left brain of yours. Sure, this hemisphere is often associated with logical thinking, analytical processing, and handling tasks that require focus and detail. But your right brain plays a role too. This hemisphere is primarily associated with creative and intuitive tasks. It plays a key role in processing visual imagery and spatial awareness, and it's also important for understanding context and the overall big picture. So now you might believe that intuition is just part of a well-functioning brain – a brain that makes well-considered choices, so intuition is just a tiny part of a big intelligent and considered analytical process in your head. Wrong! Intuition is also decided in your gut.

The moment your gut says NO – it's a no. You can unpack the details later.
THE GOOD QUOTE

Somehow intuition is linked to the brain, heart, and gut connection, also referred to as the vagus nerve.[38] The vagus what? I got you; you are probably wondering where this book is heading to! But it is important to understand a tiny bit of how our inner world functions in order to understand the dynamics we show in the outer world. The vagus nerve is like a superhighway of information running between your brain and many important organs in your body, including the heart, lungs, and gut. It's one of the longest nerves in your body and plays a crucial role in controlling automatic body functions like heartbeat, breathing, and digestion.

Think of the vagus nerve as a two-way street. It sends signals from your brain to your organs to help manage how they work, and it also sends information from your organs back to your brain. This helps your brain understand what's happening in your body and adjust as needed. For example, when you are stressed, the vagus nerve helps calm your body down by slowing your heartbeat and promoting relaxation. It's a key part of your body's relaxation response, essentially telling your body to 'chill out' when things are getting too hectic. Intuitive feelings are linked to emotional responses happening deep inside our body. Interestingly, recent research[39] on the gut has revealed that there is more communication from the gut to the brain than from the brain to the gut via the vagus nerve. This extensive gut-to-brain communication is part of what has led scientists to refer to the gut as the 'second brain', highlighting its significant role in influencing mood, well-being, and decision-making processes, often referred to as 'gut feelings'.

We might not be aware of this body-brain communication, but it is there! We might be resistant to the idea that our gut and intestines dominate a good part of our decisions, but it is a scientifically proven fact. Knowing that, it is important to acknowledge this and to better listen to our bodies and gut feelings... Something I ignored for most of my life; more on that in the last chapter of this book! Enough about difficult internal physical and mental processes. But now you know why intuition is not something to ignore; instead, it is something we should listen to more frequently and, on an unconscious level, it is a fundamental part of trusting others.

Because when we trust others, we can make great progress in our leadership skills for the following reasons:
- **Speed in decision-making:** In fast-paced environments where rapid decisions are necessary, relying solely on analysis can be impractical. Intuition allows leaders to make decisions quickly, often without needing to sift through extensive data.
- **Enhanced problem-solving:** Intuition can help leaders identify problems before they become apparent through traditional methods. This can be particularly valuable in complex situations where logical analysis might not provide all the answers.
- **Emotional insight:** Intuition is closely linked to emotional intelligence. It helps leaders sense the mood and dynamics of their team, which can guide how they motivate, manage, and support their employees effectively.
- **Personal effectiveness:** Leaders who trust their intuition often report greater job satisfaction and personal effectiveness. This self-trust can be empowering and can enhance a leader's confidence in their decision-making capabilities.

Effective and caring leaders combine their intuitive insights with data and analysis to make well-rounded decisions. They are open and transparent about their intuitive thoughts and dare to bet on them to move forward. Of course, relying only on your gut feeling can lead to biased and overly simplistic decisions. To make it to the next step of great collaboration, trust and success demands more than just your intuition. But I urge you to become more conscious about that tiny voice inside yourself, that intangible thing inside you that tells you who and what is right for you, and who or what to avoid. In a world soon to be dominated by machines, it is your intuition, gut feeling, and ethical choices that will keep humans relevant next to these far more intelligent computers. It is leadership from the heart and with a balanced IQ-EQ that will take us through the challenges organizations face. Simply trying to listen better to your gut is a first great step of becoming a caring and trustworthy leader.

STEP 2: BUILDING TRUST

Let's have a look at how collaboration is further built upon trust, seen through the eye of academic research on Leadership:[40]

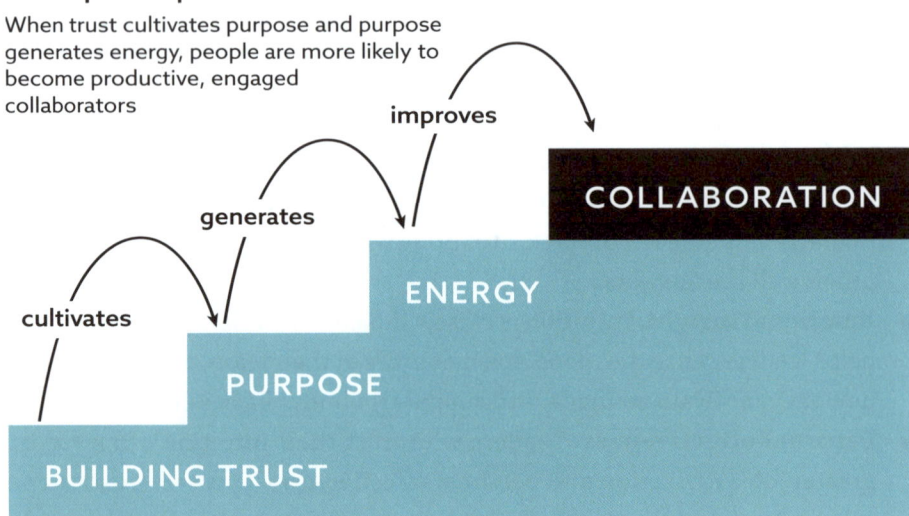

Figure 8: How to build up to productive collaboration.

Building trust and trustworthy relationships is a far better option to create productive collaboration for the long term compared to control. Collaborating to become a better performing organization cannot happen without trust among the team. Note that feeling safe is something we also rather feel in our gut than in our brain. It is a set of complex neuro-senses that give a sense of trust or distrust. Therefore it is related to your vagus nerve as explained in the previous step. The connection between the vagus nerve and feelings of safety and trust is scientifically proven,[41] primarily through its role in regulating the parasympathetic nervous system, which is often termed the 'rest and digest' system. The vagus nerve is a key component of this system, and its activation promotes a state of calm and relaxation in the body, which can contribute to feelings of safety. So, when you see, talk, meet, or hang out with your team, an unlimited number of neurons will decide whether you have managed to create a trustworthy culture. And as importantly, if people trust you!

Here are some strategies to build trust in teams:

- **It's a give and take mechanism:** Creating trustworthy environments and relationships is always about connectivity. It is a give and take mechanism, never a one-way directional action. Giving and receiving trust always involves all parties. It is about what you radiate to others and what they radiate to you. It is about a verbal and non-verbal dialogue. It is never a monologue.

- **Dare to get outside your comfort zone:** Your gut feeling tells you what your body and mind needs and who you can trust. You will automatically trust people who look and act like you. Those similar to you create an immediate feeling of trust, because they are so recognisable. But trust can also be found outside your inner circle of colleagues with whom you naturally click. In a learning process and in transformational times, psychological safety also needs to be created with others, outside your inner circle. We need to trust more people and dare to get outside our comfort zone to do that. Dare to trust your intuition and gut more than your brain to find allies – people who will help you to create that trustworthy environment. Be aware that your brain might steer you in the direction of an influential team member, for instance, but one whom you might not fully trust. So, dare to trust your gut to open up to others and to learn from others. Your gut shows you where you can learn, grow and gain trust and your brain will reward you for what you already know.

- **Creating trust happens with verbal and non-verbal communication:** You can have as many trust quotes on the wall as you want, if people feel unsafe with certain people – and unfortunately this happens more often than we think – people might pretend to follow you and collaborate, but the connection on a deeper level will be missing. There is substantial research on how non-verbal cues influence distrust among people. Non-verbal communication – such as facial expressions, body language, gestures, and vocal tones – plays a crucial role in how we perceive and interpret the intentions and trustworthiness of others. People keep up their guard if they do not feel safe. And with their guard up, you never fully connect on deeper levels, something necessary to reach that level of productive collaboration. Remember that you can talk about trust or being a trustworthy leader, but if people don't instinctively believe you, you will not truly be trusted.

- **Equality and respect:** What helps tremendously to create trust is when people feel equal and/or seen and respected. But trust also means that team members also feel safe to take risks, are allowed to make mistakes without punishment, speak up with ideas and questions, and report mistakes without fear of sanctions or humiliation. Respect is something again that is most felt, not said. If words of respect are pronounced, but you feel those words are not genuine, you will not feel respected.

A type of coaching I have never experienced but am fascinated with is horse-assisted coaching. In a Dutch audio episode of the CARE Principles podcast[42] I had the pleasure of talking to Joost Callens, ex-CEO of a sustainable building company called Durabrik. Joost talked about how he followed many leadership trainings and coaching. One in particular stood out: to lead a horse and let it execute commands purely on voice guidance. He explained how the coachee is encouraged to establish a connection with the horse through observation, grooming, and non-verbal communication. Building trust and rapport with the horse is essential for the coaching process, as the horse is not impressed by the size, gender, business card, smart outfit, or fancy car of the person in front of it! Horses are highly attuned to non-verbal cues and can sense the coachee's emotions, intentions, and energy. The horse's reactions to the coachee's actions, body language, and communication style serve as valuable feedback for your leadership style. Horses respond to genuine behaviour. The valuable lesson to learn from horses is that they can sense incongruence – when someone's emotions do not match their actions. This lesson is crucial for leaders, emphasising the need for authenticity in building trust and credibility with their teams. This type of coaching class is high on my wish list!

- **Lead by example:** Leaders should model the behaviour they wish to see. This includes admitting their own mistakes, showing vulnerability, and treating every question or concern as valuable. By doing so, leaders signal to employees that it's safe to do the same.

- **Set clear and transparent expectations:** Clarify roles, responsibilities, and the behaviours expected from team members. When people know what's expected of them, they're more likely to feel secure in their ability to contribute effectively. Be transparent about their roles and expectations – and to other team members too – as that leaves no room for guesswork or preferential treatment. If people or departments get preferential treatment, it kills trust.

- **Cut out the negative influences:** When you have established trust, remain vigilant as one new team member can change the culture and influence the trustworthy environment you have built. Organizational culture is a strange and intangible thing that can create low workforce morale overnight. Decisive action against negative behaviours is necessary as it reinforces the values that the organization stands for. It sends a clear message about what is acceptable and what is not, encouraging others to behave in ways that align with the organization's values. Every process of talking to someone about possible unaccepted leadership needs to be done with care and consciousness of the damage this can bring to the person, their environment, and the business. Exceptions cannot be made if you want an engaged team on all levels.

- **No exceptions permitted:** Double standards unfortunately live in many organizations, specifically when the 'disruptors' are in leading and successful positions. Many times, I witnessed CEOs protecting toxic leaders because they managed large revenues or important client relationships, for instance. Everybody had to live by the rules, except for these managers. In the short term, these practices can be understood – nobody wants to jeopardise revenue or potential loss of clients – but in the long haul it erodes the trust and confidence of your team in you as a leader. Disruptive individuals can significantly impact the team's effectiveness. Their behaviour can cause distractions, reduce collaboration, and even lead to valuable employees leaving the organization. Moreover, it gives these toxic leaders a signal that they can get away with it, and it becomes a lifestyle that they continue throughout their careers. Most toxic leaders grow in their power and belief that what they do is right. The fact that nobody holds them accountable and that they feel protected by their management gives them a signal to continue. A wrong attitude, unfortunately, still spotted in too many companies!

Let's have a look now at how purpose is an important stepping stone towards more productive collaboration.

STEP 3: DEFINING AND CULTIVATING YOUR ORGANIZATIONAL PURPOSE

In Japan they have a beautiful word for finding your purpose, both on a personal and on an organizational level and it is called finding your 'ikigai'. Ikigai is a Japanese concept that refers to one's reason for being or finding your true sense of purpose in life.

Your ikigai lies in the intersection of:
- what you love
- what you are good at
- what the world needs
- what you can be paid for.

This Japanese concept suggests that finding where these four elements converge can lead to fulfilment, happiness, and balance. Ikigai is essentially about finding joy and satisfaction in life through purpose. Isn't this what organizations should also strive for?

How do academics define an organizational purpose? There are many academic definitions to be found; I am happy to share this one by my favourite, Professor Robben,[43] with whom I collaborate at the Business University Nyenrode:

'Organizational purpose is the motivating force moving, guiding, and delivering the organization to a perceived goal. It is the driving force, the fuel, the bond, the intangible link that pulls the organization together to achieve success.'

When you're surrounded by people who share a passionate commitment around a common purpose, anything is possible.

HOWARD SCHULTZ (FORMER CEO OF STARBUCKS)

In my own words, as I am clearly no academic, I would say that an organizational purpose is a goal that gets people out of bed, and that drives your organization. Purpose goes beyond financial gains. A purpose is about wanting to leave a positive social and/or environmental impact. The concept of such a purpose is gaining traction; you start to see it among leading companies who understand that there is more to business than just financial gains. But can a purpose make money too? Does it pay the bills? Is it worthwhile defining a purpose? According to a Deloitte study and the World Economic Forum,[44] crafting a purpose pays off big time. Businesses with a clear purpose do better, while protecting people and planet! Deloitte's study amongst 400 American companies revealed the following insights:

- Companies with a clear purpose are more likely to inspire trust.
- Those with a strong and effective purpose strategy see the returns.
- 28% of consumers declared to have stopped buying products based upon ethical concerns.
- 73% of investors believe that a company's social and environmental efforts contribute to returns.

This is totally in line with my own experience. I had the chance to help several companies find and craft their purpose, an exercise that is always done with the whole company or at least that is discussed with all employees as it is not a good idea to craft a purpose only with the management team and then throw it into the organization as an agreed fact. Take your time to find and define your organizational purpose and share it with all your employees to get full alignment on it. Fulfilling the purpose will go so much more smoothly afterwards as it is a shared goal for everyone involved, and not a top-down decision that is being pushed through the organization. Moreover, it is also nice to share it with external parties and find collaboration with others on shared purpose goals. The willingness to make social and environmental impact together is the only way to make impact at a fast pace!

Many leaders I talk about a purpose with are afraid they cannot make a big statement. They are quick to tell me they are not Patagonia, *'We are in business to save our home planet'*. A client of mine had lost some of his best employees due to a lack of purpose. He knew he needed to offer his employees more than just a job as a real estate agent to keep them happy, empowered and engaged. Still, he had major doubts about how his real estate agency could find a true and honest purpose. Luckily, he understood that making money was simply not good enough anymore, for many talented people. Before losing more of them, he was brave enough to decide to dedicate time to the process of thinking and crafting an organizational purpose that fitted his organization and that engaged his people. It is important to craft a purpose close to your heart, and it doesn't matter if it is small, local, and just matters to you and your employees. If it is something that keeps you and your team inspired, it is a great purpose! However, there are some pitfalls to consider when discovering your organizational purpose:

- **Walk the talk:** Don't create a purpose solely for marketing reasons. A purpose is not a marketing or communication tool to make you look better. Purpose-washing is as bad as greenwashing, and your staff will be the first to know and condemn you when you don't really mean what you say. And it is not just your employees who will be disappointed. In this ever-connected world, bad news travels fast and consumers will find out when you try to deceive them through purpose-washing. We are already seeing court actions on a global scale against greenwashing. Total France faced legal action for greenwashing communication.[45] In advertising showing wind turbines and solar panels, they claimed to work hard on renewable energy. The company is planning a massive fossil fuel expansion, increasing its production of polluting gas, and relying on as-yet-unproven technology, while avoiding meaningful action to reduce emissions this decade. But also, social, or inclusive claims made by companies are quickly taken down when employees reveal the reality within company walls. Starbucks[46] landed in a LGBTQ+ public storm when trans members of their staff revealed how gender-affirming care benefits in the company's healthcare plan could be dropped if trans people planned to unionise.

- **Make your purpose authentic and honest:** A strong organizational purpose strategy identifies a company's most important issues. Often it is related to the CEO's convictions and beliefs. A well-intended purpose establishes a holistic, differentiated approach that motivates the employees, drives the organizational culture, and helps to hire new employees with the right spirit for the cause. The more authentic the purpose, the more it will drive your company on the inside. But it doesn't stop there; as mentioned before, it is spotted by consumers and can help to turn your brand into a love brand, a brand that is passed on with mouth-to-mouth advertising among like-minded people. Your purpose can be something small, very local, and even insignificant to others. If it motivates the leaders to get out of bed for it, it will work for your organization.

- **Collaborate with others to realise your purpose:** Whatever social or environmental purpose you have, reaching out to others to go faster, care more, have more impact together is better. Inside or outside your industry, find harmonious allies to join the fight for that good cause your organization stands for. Once you have established an engaging purpose, see if you can collaborate with your clients, for instance. It can lead to great co-created actions with more impact!

- **Measure your impact:** Not everyone in the organization will fully align with the purpose; for certain people, working from a purpose matters more than for others. Again, generational thinking will probably show you different results. When you track the progress and impact you make, it is a great tool to learn and get insight into what is working and what is not. It helps to motivate your staff for future progress, and it makes your purpose tangible and real, far from a marketing and brand image-driven campaign. It helps you to create a culture in which failure is part of success and you carefully measure the steps towards realising your organizational purpose. Adding a question like 'Who among you leaves you feeling a greater sense of purpose in your work after an interaction?' to your purpose survey can help you identify the departments that are running behind on purpose-driven working and train these departments further on this subject. By involving your workforce in tracking the success of purpose-driven work, you can monitor if younger generations value purpose more or not, and act accordingly with sub-groups of your employees. In the CARE Scan, differences are always spotted in the importance of a purpose for different age groups, gender, and departments, so the more you know, the more you can address the issues!

- **The Pareto Principle:**[47] This implies that 80% of the sense of purpose within the organization is generated by just 20% of its leaders and that these leaders have, among other things, a significantly better record of employee retention than the rest. Understanding that purpose progress is often made in baby steps, in fussy processes of going forward and backward at the same time. Accept also that not all people will be as enthusiastic about your purpose plan; it will speak more loudly to some, and that is okay. Finally, a warning for the purpose doubters: don't judge a purpose with your calculator in your head. Purpose comes from the heart and starts as an honest attempt to do right. The effect it will have on your team comes next. The effect it can have on your clients is secondary. Don't mistake purpose for a business goal; they are fundamentally different!

In conclusion, having an organizational purpose might be highly motivational for some, and of no importance for others. But there is substantial research indicating that having a well-defined organizational purpose can contribute significantly to a company's success. Purpose-driven companies often experience benefits such as enhanced employee engagement, stronger customer loyalty, improved stakeholder relations, more profitability and better overall performance. What are you waiting for? Start that exercise now and think about what keeps you going beyond status and financial success.

STEP 4: ENERGY AND FLOW HELP

When you follow your intuition, you create a trustworthy environment, and you have crafted a meaningful purpose, I can assure you that your team will be full of energy, and teamwork will flow in a natural way! When people feel recognised and have the idea that they matter, they will come to work energetic and enthusiastic about their day-to-day job. When you accomplish this, your organization will thrive. This is what I learned from Jan Bommerez,[48] an author and coach, specialised in letting go and trauma healing. Jan is an autodidact, he studied for most of his life to handle his own traumas and issues and started to write books and video courses about his insights, as he had trouble finding adequate help on his transformational journey.

His interpretation of the flow theory, as originally formulated by Professor Csikszentmihalyi,[49] emphasises the state where individuals are fully immersed and engaged in activities that are both challenging and rewarding. In one of Jan's books, he adapts the flow concept to the business world, suggesting that achieving flow in professional activities can lead to greater creativity, productivity, collaboration, and satisfaction. This makes total sense as only teams who trust each other, and are working together on that joined purpose, get the energy of moving forward together. It is a beautiful state of mind and action to witness within organizations that have that energy aligned. When teams reach this state of flow and energy, work doesn't feel laborious; instead, there's an effortless progression of actions towards a goal. Work feels like play when there is clarity in the roles of each team member, and when everyone has the capacity to turn problems into solutions.

Bommerez argues that understanding and fostering the conditions that lead to flow can greatly benefit both individuals and organizations. By creating environments that encourage flow, businesses can thrive, adapt, and innovate more successfully. This flow mindset can be helped by the environment and the way the office has been designed. Please stop building those open-space offices as a multitude of research[50] has indicated that it is not productive for most people and can even have detrimental effects on workers' well-being. Sure, these lofty offices are beautiful to see – I understand the architectural and design aspect of them – but they have a horrible effect on concentration and focus. Some studies even suggest they are a killer of collaboration![51]

One aspect of keeping the energy flowing among people is to have an office that caters for synchronous working, with great spaces that enhance collaboration, fun and play! But also asynchronous working spots for those moments that people need to work separately, quietly and with great focus. Finally, exciting things are already happening with the construction of smart and sustainable buildings. These are buildings that measure many data sets like energy and water usage and cleaning costs. Today there are experiments tracking the favourite coffees and coffee breaks of employees. Deloitte Amsterdam uses an app to help employees with their schedules for the day. To increate well-being, employees are guided to a sitting or standing desk, work booth, meeting room or 'concentration room'. These experiments might come across as scary and like 'big brother' is watching you, but they certainly can help optimise energy flows when executed with care.

But flow is about more than the office space you work in. How remarkable are teams whose approach to work goes from effort and control towards more effortless involvement, letting go and trusting people. This shift allows for a deeper engagement with tasks, fostering an environment where innovation and peak performance can thrive. The theory implies that when leaders and teams operate in a state of flow, they are not only more efficient and effective but also more fulfilled and motivated, leading to a positive impact on overall business success. Teams and team leaders who understand this create a sense of belonging on the work floor and motivation peaks.

I would like to make a remark here about the plotting of people in behavioural personality frameworks like MBTI, DISC, and Insights Discovery. All the organizations I have ever worked with are fans of these types of definitions of people, and I understand this. I would just like to warn about the way it limits people. I have so often heard people tell others: 'I don't do that, because I am yellow.' Or 'I will never accept that behaviour as I am blue.' People accept this label as a something final and written in stone, while we can all evolve and learn how do things differently, even if it is not part of our basic skillset or character, right? At least this is what I believe! I believe we can all embrace a growth mindset and not a fixed mindset. A growth mindset, a concept developed by psychologist Carol Dweck,[52] is a mindset where people believe that their abilities and intelligence can be developed through dedication, hard work, and learning from experiences.

So, continue to have fun learning about yourself and what colour or role you have in the team, but don't forget to be open and open-minded to learn from others. Similar thoughts about energy can be made in line with personality traits. If your team has too many innovators and not enough sceptics your transformational plans might not be successful. You need everyone and the more diverse your team is on all levels, the better your organization will be prepared for the future.

A final remark: energy can vary from day to day and even hourly, because it is under the influence of so many internal and external aspects of people. Never stop asking your team how they feel. That leads me to the last step for a great, successful, and productive collaboration: communication and comprehension. Two very different things that are fundamental to kick-start your collaborative mindset!

STEP 5: COMMUNICATION AND COMPREHENSION

As mentioned before, individuals are increasingly awarded greater responsibility, self-direction, and self-leadership for their own job pursuits. As such, they will be asked to rely on their own skills for most aspects of their work, not only including technical skills, but soft skills, too, such as work ethic, attitude, communication and interpersonal skills, emotional intelligence, and several other social attributes. Soft skills are the new hard skills and will become a cornerstone of the future workforce. The CARE Principles are often regarded as soft skills, but one can argue about whether that is true. I personally see nothing soft in collaboration or agility, for instance. Are soft skills not the most difficult to learn in business?

The importance of these soft skills is often undervalued, states the 'Unlocking the Future of People and Organizations' report.[53] The report mentions that there is far less training provided for soft skills, with the assumption upheld that everyone knows and understands the importance of these less-tangible skills. But claiming more of the largely untapped potential here, and really investing in personal accountability, interpersonal negotiation skills, adaptability and flexibility, creative thinking, and inclusion can increase performance, and is a great way to prepare yourself for the future.

However, let's talk about the art of communication. A skill we all believe we have mastered. Still, in reality it creates the biggest problems in the world, even leading to wars! Many leaders who have status and a certain level of power are good at talking. So good that, quite often, you witness that they have lost the ability to listen. They might hear you, but they don't listen. Each sentence you say is an opportunity for them to turn the conversation to themselves and continue what is in essence a monologue. Being a good leader is always about a dialogue, never about a monologue. Communication is about training your ability to send and to receive. To listen and truly hear. Not to listen to solely respond. When you listen to conversations between couples in restaurants, for instance, it's staggering how often they talk to each other, not with each other. Two streams of words flowing next to one another, rarely finding connection. But it's not just couple talk that can be improved. Communication and comprehension on the work floor has plenty of flaws too.

Leadership transformation and reaching a high level of productive collaboration needs one final ingredient and that is communication. Communication takes courage and time. It seems to be one of the easiest things humans do, and still, it is where things go wrong most of the time! Many conflicts arise from poor communication. The comprehension of your communication might be lacking. People listen carefully but simply don't understand what you say. Sometimes they fear asking what you really mean, as asking questions or admitting that you didn't fully understand the boss's demands could come across as 'stupid'.

Communication can go wrong in many ways:
- People hear you but don't listen.
- People's perception of your words and actions differ from your intent.
- Leaders must 'walk the talk' and 'talk the walk'. That means they need to communicate who they are and the intent of their actions in clear, unambiguous ways.
- When leaders leave employees guessing, those guesses often take a negative cast.

- Being unable to keep confidential information to yourself and using that as a 'power play' is something I witnessed too often, unfortunately. It erodes trust among team members.
- Competence-based trust can be problematic, too, if leaders are unwilling to admit that they don't know everything.

Good and clear communication is about:
- being open-minded
- being honest
- daring to show your vulnerable side when needed
- 'us' and not 'I'; showing that you act in the interests of others – and not just yourself – is crucial to stimulate collaboration
- daring to say you do not understand, or do not have the answer or solution
- verbal skills and non-verbal signals
- taking time
- spreading consistent messages across all your communication tools
- taking time to understand whether they comprehended your message
- balancing the act of sending and receiving messages
- understanding that sometimes it is not the moment for a particular remark or feedback. Timing is everything, especially for comprehension.

Communication is key to bringing and keeping your team members on board. Good communication can resolve many potential misunderstandings and conflicts before they escalate. This is more important than ever and it's essential to open dialogue, especially around difficult subjects like mental health. By addressing such issues openly, leaders can help those who are struggling in silence and promote a culture of openness and support. Clear, consistent communication is a foundation for building and maintaining strong, cohesive teams. Good and effective communication is a two-way action. It demands proper care and attention to make sure the comprehension is there. Way too often managers believe that if they simply say what needs to be done, it will be done.

Comprehension fosters trust and respect, as it shows that the parties are actively listening and valuing each other's perspectives, leaving time and room for dialogue and feedback. In summary, comprehension turns the act of merely transmitting information into true communication, which is a critical tool for achieving goals, resolving issues, and creating trust and bonds.

> **I used to think communication was the key until I realised comprehension is. You can communicate all you want, but if they don't understand you, it's silent chaos.**
>
> **THE GOOD QUOTE**

Communication and comprehension are about realising that your CARE leadership transformation is about engagement and commitment. Invite your team to the table to collaborate, communicate and co-create, so together you can find ways to achieve your objectives. Excellent and productive collaboration is about building the future while engaging the whole team!

PODCAST INTERVIEW

WITH ERIK-JAN MARES, CEO ZEEMAN.

Erik-Jan Mares, the CEO of Zeeman, a Dutch family-owned brand of textile stores across 8 European countries, is a very inspirational leader. His time at Zeeman marks a period of transformative leadership, emphasising sustainability, European expansion, and online growth. I met Erik-Jan some years ago when I inspired the long-term strategy of the company with some keynotes and strategic help. But even before meeting anyone at this family-owned company, I was impressed by them. Their brand, marketing strategies and communication is all so amazing, unique, and successful. I wrote a case about them in my first book and also had the pleasure of interviewing Caroline Van Turenhout, the marketing director. Check this Dutch interview here [54] as they are also a true leader in marketing.

> **I'll let you in on a secret. I like to spend more time with younger people than with people my own age, for a lot of reasons. I spend a lot of time with younger people to just understand them and get inspired.**
>
> **ERIK-JAN MARES, CEO ZEEMAN**

My interview with Erik-Jan confirmed what I already knew, but more so. Erik-Jan opened up and explained why he became a better version of himself and a better leader. He also shared what he does at Zeeman to continue his personal transition, but also that of his organization. Erik-Jan Mares' leadership tips are crucial:

- Tip 1: The most important leadership tip by far is that if you are not connected to yourself, and if you're not dealing with yourself, then you can't lead yourself. And how can you lead others if you can't lead yourself? So, tip 1 is to make sure that you understand yourself, because it all starts with you.
- Tip 2: Listen to this feeling in your stomach. Sometimes it can be a warning signal; sometimes these feelings can be uncomfortable. But this discomfort means that you're learning. When you are learning, it means that you're leaving something behind, and you're learning something new, and it makes you feel unsettled, and uncomfortable.

Make sure you listen to the full interview. I honestly could have spent a whole day listening to this bright, empathetic, fun, and unconventional leader. Scan the QR code to listen to the CARE Principles podcast.

https://spotifyanchor-web.app.link/e/2WTeEBwtgMb

COLLABORATION EXERCISES

Intuition: TALK TO YOUR GUT

Solo exercise
Awareness exercise. Think about a recent situation in which you felt your gut feeling was very clearly telling you something.
Ask yourself:
- What happened?
- In what situation did this happen?
- What was the trigger to make you feel this? Was it a remark from a colleague? Was it a certain atmosphere or an energy that caused it? Was it non-verbal communication from the other? What did you sense?
- Did you listen to it, or did you ignore it?
- Did you dare to act upon it?
- Imagine you didn't, what would you do next time if you are in a similar situation?

Purpose of this exercise: a continuous learning process of awareness of noticing and acting on your gut feeling. It is a process of growing your self-confidence and trusting your unconscious and conscious feelings. Allowing your intuition to become a part of your decision-making and leadership style.

Trust: HONESTY CHALLENGE

Duo exercise
Think about a colleague you don't really know well from inside or outside your department. During a coffee break, or lunch, or afternoon walk, dare to talk to this person and ask if they are open to listening to a personal story, experience, doubt, worry, fuck-up you want to share with them. After sharing your story, ask for their feedback, their perspective on the story, maybe just their compassion or whatever you would like to get out of this situation. Wait and see their reaction. There is a good chance this person will respond in a positive and caring way, and you will see your personal issue with a fresh pair of eyes. You can do this exercise as often as you wish, with as many people as you wish.

Purpose of this exercise: to open up and show vulnerability and through that create psychological safety for yourself, but also for others. Importantly, you will also learn a different perspective than yours on the personal story you shared. By bonding on a deeper level with your colleague, you created an ally and buddy for more productive collaboration, even with someone far from your department.

Purpose: FIND YOUR WHY

Team exercise
Find your organizational purpose by imagining that money and growth and profit were taken care of, so nobody had to focus on the economic side of the business. In that situation, ask yourselves the question: what is your organization's reason for existing? What is your contribution to this world? What positive impact do you want to make with the company? What gives you energy? What is your reason for existing? Ask your team members to do the same exercise. Come together and share your thoughts.

Purpose of this exercise: here it is simple, to find your organizational purpose and your why – finding out why you do the job, or what the higher purpose of the organization is, beyond economic reasons. A purpose will give you a reason to connect, empower and engage your workforce.

Energy: ENERGY FINDER

Team exercise
Write down on post-its all the roles, tasks, responsibilities, and behaviour/energy that are needed in your team or division. Take one post-it per task and stick them all to a wall. Stand together and read them carefully one by one, in silence. Notice inside (gut!) which of the post-its is totally 'you' – what suits you best, what is calling out to you. After a few minutes, when everyone has read and chosen in silence, one by one pick the post-its you selected from the wall. Of course, some post-its will be taken by more people – let's have a conversation! Maybe create buddies to collaborate on one task? And maybe some of the post-its will be left on the wall – what about those? Discuss openly why nobody is attracted to those, or why it is always

the same people who volunteer for the shitty jobs? Maybe take co-ownership of the more annoying tasks to split the burden. You will learn from these discussions and find out together how to solve this – by turn-taking, for instance.

Purpose of the exercise: to divide all the team tasks, roles, and energies between the team members to create the optimal strength in the team and let people work in their flow. Use all the different energies and qualities of the team members in the best possible way to reach a state of productive collaboration.

Communication: EXPLICIT DRAWING EXERCISE

Duo exercise
Place two chairs back-to-back and sit with a colleague with your backs towards each other. Both take a paper and a pen. One draws a simple drawing, without showing it to the other. Then he/she explains the drawing with words to the colleague. The drawing cannot be shown, only described. The colleague cannot ask questions and must draw what they understood from the directions that were given verbally. At the end, compare the two drawings with your colleague.

Purpose of this exercise: Rarely are both drawings the same! It is a good exercise in understanding different perspectives. It is a great test for your instruction skills: what is the tempo of your instructions? How much detail did you go into in instructions? For your colleague it is a great exercise to test their comprehension skills.

Can't wait to read about AGILITY?

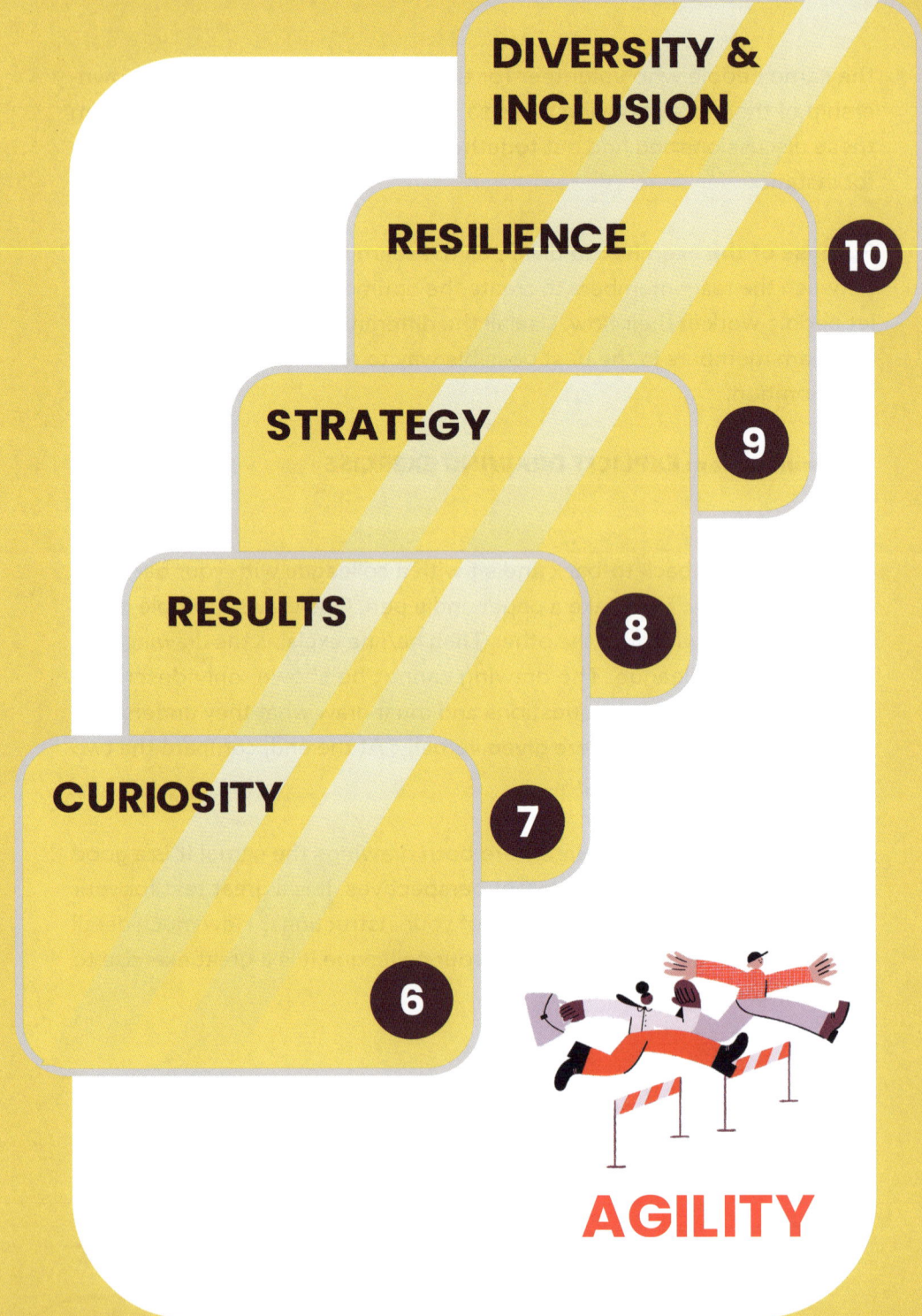

PLAY SECTION 6
AGILITY IS NEEDED

The second strategic Principle that companies need to sharpen is all about speed, reactivity, flexibility, diversification, innovation, and resilience. It is very important to train your reactivity, as it prepares you for a rapidly changing world. The speed with which these changes will become necessary will only increase; simply check out how ChatGPT – launched on November 30th, 2022 – achieved 1 million users within just five days of launching, which made it the fastest-growing application in history at that time. There is no use in giving you an exact number of users today, as they increase at the speed of light!

Agility is so much more than technology and AI, right? Agility and innovation go hand in hand as when you don't look forward, interpret new consumer trends, respond to changes in customer demands, make your offer more sustainable, and invent new product or services, you die. But because artificial intelligence is such a game-changer, I'll explain about AI and leadership. What is regenerative artificial intelligence? ChatGPT4 – a popular artificial intelligence powered open AI platform – says AI is like a computer brain that can learn, make decisions, and solve problems in a way that somewhat resembles how humans think. Instead of being programmed to do just one specific task, AI can use large amounts of data and experience to improve over time and adapt to new situations. It's used in many everyday technologies, such as smartphone voice assistants, online recommendation systems like those on shopping sites, and self-driving cars. AI helps these systems understand and predict patterns to make decisions that are usually informed by human behaviour.

There are huge debates going on about the future impact of AI on humanity. Look up bright people like Mo Gawdat, Yuval Noah Harari or Elon Musk and listen to their thoughts and opinions on AI. I can assure you it is quite scary.

In this world where many things could tilt us in the wrong direction, generative AI is by far the number one topic that should be on the agenda of world leaders. The ethical side of computer intelligence, laws and regulations is urgently needed. One thing is for sure, I am not nearly intelligent enough to give the answers to that urgent ethical problem. I can only hope the evil powers in society will be outnumbered by the caring forces of good. Let's dive into the impact AI will have on leadership.

A first impact is that knowledge is no longer of the utmost importance it used to be. People who climbed the corporate ladder were often the ones who had more knowledge than others. Today a six-year-old child can put pretty much any question to an AI-powered application or platform and replicate its answer. The answer will be more complete and correct than the knowledge of many people today. This will have a huge impact on who will make the decisions and steer the discussions within teams. Brilliant people who lack digital skills will become dinosaurs. They will have trouble adapting to their new status among teams where their opinions could be questioned by computer narratives. Generative AI can make average people look very smart. ChatGPT 4 can explain very complex things in language that is very simple and easy to understand. That is a skill we once paid a lot of money for as not many people had that skill. How will this affect the promotion of people? Which people will be the best in your leadership teams? How can you deal with these evolving workplace dynamics?

Let's look at some key strategies to make the most of an AI-fuelled talent approach:
- **Focus on human-centric skills:** Emphasise and develop skills that are uniquely human and less likely to be replicated by AI, such as creativity, critical thinking, emotional intelligence, and interpersonal communication. These skills will become more valuable as AI takes over more routine and knowledge-driven tasks.
- **Lifelong learning:** We have said it before, but we need to stress it: encourage a culture of lifelong learning! As AI will constantly evolve, the ability to adapt and learn new skills will be crucial. Providing opportunities for employees to engage in continuous professional development can help them stay relevant in their fields.

- **Ethical leadership:** Promote leaders who not only understand the technical aspects of AI but also the ethical implications. Leaders should be trained to use AI responsibly, ensuring that its implementation supports inclusivity and diversity within the organization.
- **Job redesign:** As AI will automate more and more tasks, redesign jobs to make them more meaningful and satisfying for humans. This can involve integrating AI tools to handle mundane aspects of a job, allowing employees to focus on more complex and rewarding tasks.
- **Enhance collaboration between you and the machines:** Brace yourself for a future in which AI chips will probably be integrated into our bodies. Yes, I kid you not, that is what innovative labs are working on. For now, embrace AI and encourage collaborations that leverage both human creativity and AI efficiency. For example, creative professionals can use AI to explore new ideas and solutions, while relying on their human judgment to make final decisions.
- **Transparent communication:** Instead of frightening employees if they might lose their jobs to computers, maintain open channels of communication about how AI is being used in the workplace. This helps in managing employee expectations and reducing fears related to AI and automation.
- **Foster an agile and innovation-minded culture:** Create an environment where experimenting with AI solutions is encouraged. This can lead to innovations that not only improve productivity but also open new roles and opportunities for employees.

These strategies not only help in promoting individuals within a company but also ensure that the workforce remains competitive and prepared for the changes brought about by AI technologies. By focusing on these aspects, organizations can create a supportive and dynamic environment that harnesses the best of both human and artificial intelligence. Fighting the new is mostly a waste of energy; embrace it and you will see that your talented people will help you leverage it to your advantage, and for the growth of your teams and organizations. If this is blowing your mind, I can only advise you to ask your younger team members – or children, if you are a solo entrepreneur like me – to share their ideas and thoughts on what's hot and what is not in new tools, apps, and programs to help your work.

POSSIBLE AGILITY HURDLES

Independently from technological changes and disruptions, the two main hurdles we witness within a company are linked to people and processes. Many people don't like change, and they are frightened of changes that might occur in their routines. Changes that might lead to mistakes, that might lead to them getting into trouble. Considered in that light, it is easy to understand why any procedural change is looked at with suspicion. 'Will I be unable to adapt to the new way of doing things, will I lose my job, how will I keep my power and how will I be rewarded?' are among the common fears people express. Demanding a flexible attitude from your staff only works if they trust the organization, if they know that they will not be punished for the try-outs they test. Trust and reliability are very important assets and part of the next strategic Principle. Asking for and demonstrating an agile mindset without trust is difficult.

But your employees are not the only reason why your much-needed organizational change processes are unsuccessful. Change processes are often poorly thought out and badly communicated. Some new ways of working are little more than old wine in new bottles. Fancy wording and fancy concepts are unleashed on old hierarchical structures and management hopes for the best as to how people deal with it. Suddenly calling teams 'squads' won't be enough to introduce an agile way of working. Some people might try to boycott newly proposed structures, agile ways of working or changed procedures; there are often good reasons to hold onto the existing ones. In most cases, finding a good balance of what works for the company and its staff, while being open and evolving towards a more contemporary organization demands time, an adaptive mindset, compassion, and flexibility.

If you are looking at changing your organizational structure to become more flexible, faster, and more adapted to today's needs, I totally recommend the book and knowledge of the Dutch organization Corporate Rebels.[55] They talk to leaders worldwide in all sectors who explain new organizational structures and workplace innovations. The Copenhagen Institute for Future Studies[56] predicts in one of their papers on the future of work that the next generation of companies will find inspiration in DOAs – Decentralised Autonomous Organizations. DAOs are member-owned organizations without any centralised leadership. Instead, they use software algorithms, rules, and manifestos to facilitate and sustain relationships, and offer hyper-agile work-models, therewith providing a sense of direction and purpose.

In this chapter, I have selected five more steps to make your teams more reactive, agile, and mentally resilient. I need to talk about diversity and inclusion too, as the world outside the company walls still looks very different from inside the company walls. Progress has been made in the DEI field, but it is slow, so in the podcast episode at the end of this chapter, I am happy to get wise insights from the talented multi-entrepreneur Hanan Challouki on this topic.

HOW AGILE ARE ORGANIZATIONS? THE CARE SCAN BENCHMARK STUDY REVEAL

Figure 9: Care Scan agility scores.

In the benchmark study, we saw that collaboration results were not great. When you look at the agility scores, you cannot really say they are fabulous. The overall agility score is 56%. Internal agility scores are the second worst: 54%. The agility score for the planet is the worst with 52%. Some of Ivox's questions around internal agility are about how much freedom employees receive to innovate.

- 43% of employees state that they are encouraged to work according to existing procedures.
- 64% of employees indicated that their employer helps them to keep up with the latest developments.
- 45% of employees state that none of the rules and regulations vary for individuals. This is totally understandable from an organizational point of

view, but it goes against certain people's individual need to perform at their best. Clarity and transparency about these rules and regulations within an organization often are lacking. I engaged in a conversation with a facility manager of a big German logistics brand. She said that certain managers granted their people flexible working hours and home work, but her manager didn't. When I asked her why she wasn't allowed to work from home after Covid and others were, she told me she had no clue. Her job can be done from home. I suppose that if I had talked to her manager, it is likely that a very good reason was at the base of this decision. The management must have forgotten to communicate openly and transparently about it, leaving employees guessing as to why certain departments received a privilege like home work. Colleagues start to envy others and employee morale can drop. A pity, because clear, honest, and transparent communication on this topic can avoid this.

- The overall topic of innovation scores is worrying as well:
    - 31% state that innovation is not their strong suit.
    - 33% state they don't have an opinion on this topic.
    - 37% somewhat agree that their company invests in new products and NPD processes.
- Finally, a last statistic from this benchmark study: 35% of employees say that when there is a vacancy, their organization does not look for profiles that would improve diversity in their company (e.g. non-native speakers, people with a migration background or disability).

Do you urgently need to learn how to improve your agility? With no further delay, read on for the five leadership steps to remain or become more agile.

THE 5 STEPS TO DEMONSTRATE AGILITY IN LEADERSHIP

STEP 6: CURIOSITY

Curiosity is generally considered a positive trait because it drives learning, innovation, and understanding. However, it can be perceived as negative in certain contexts due to cultural, social, and organizational reasons. Excessive curiosity about others' personal lives can be seen as intrusive or disrespectful.

When curiosity crosses the boundary into prying, it can damage relationships and trust. That is of course not what we mean when we like to stimulate your curiosity as an important step in an agile mindset. Bosses and leaders today have that position because they have a certain skillset combined with knowledge, experience and sometimes charisma. People who are good at things are often promoted to become the manager of a team. But there are two important things we often see when this happens:
- People with a very good skillset and talent for their job are not necessarily good bosses. They often lack leadership skills to manage teams. This creates frustration at both ends of the team: the manager is frustrated his people don't listen to him, and the team is frustrated as the promoted colleague lacks qualities to stimulate and engage people.
- Once the promotion is made, managers are considered managers, and few organizations continue to offer training in leadership. So, the newly promoted boss is on his own to figure out how to lead teams. As it is not stimulated by the organization and that person is on top of the organizational ladder, they lose their curiosity and eagerness to learn. Their heads are filled with other worries.

Good leaders however remain curious and eager to learn. Often, we see people in positions of power who have lost the ability to learn and remain curious. The higher they climb on the corporate or power ladder, the more they lose touch with reality and end up in ivory towers. In these towers, they surround themselves with 'yes men', people who know how their leaders think and who are hired to confirm their thoughts and actions. I can imagine that when you read this, you think that it is short-sighted and that it has not happened to you. I agree, it is short-sighted, but I deal with these types of leaders more often than you can imagine. I challenge you to question yourself and the people around you in your management team. The more comfort they give you, the more it feels like a warm blanket to crawl under. As a leader, you often think that it is nice to deal with a team that understands you, confirms your thoughts, and acts on your words.

Sure, that is fine! But think again. There is something strange about power and being in a comfortable place. Physical, mental, financial comfort creates a dominant position with a lot of respect and power over others. It takes courage and sobriety not to start to believe in your own power play. As mentioned before, leaders who have access to better coffee and exclusive catering in their office, who don't need to look for a parking spot or have the perks of a driver, who do not need to do their own grocery shopping, who spend their free time with like-minded people, and who get paid a generous bonus for steering the organization towards more growth, simply like to be surrounded with people who say YES to most of their ideas.

The tale of 'The emperor's new clothes' refers to a situation where people are afraid to criticise something or speak out against an obvious problem or falsehood, often because they do not want to appear out of step with the majority or are adhering to social norms or authority. This collective denial or wilful ignorance is seen more than often among CEOs and management teams. Leaders who remain curious and who keep in touch – not only with their own workforce and clients, but with sides of society that they do not necessarily frequent often – are often leaders who dare to have critical managers in their teams. Lifelong learning and being open to better understanding not only of the technological changes in society, but also of cultural shifts like the woke movement, me-too revelations, and political and societal polarisations is crucial to keeping your antennae developed. With the internet and information bubbles we all live in, it takes serious effort to get out of your comfort zone. But I ask you to try it.

Curiosity and a commitment to lifelong learning are crucial qualities for leadership for several reasons:

- **Adaptability to change:** The business landscape is constantly evolving, driven by technological advancements, market dynamics, and cultural shifts. Leaders who are curious and open to learning are more adaptable and able to navigate through these changes effectively. They seek to understand new trends and technologies, which enables them to make informed decisions and keep their organizations competitive.
- **Problem solving capabilities:** Curiosity drives leaders to question the status quo and explore new possibilities. This exploration fosters innovation as it leads to the discovery of unique solutions to challenges. Leaders who learn continuously can draw from a broader knowledge base and diverse perspectives, enhancing their ability to solve problems creatively.
- **Empathy**: Lifelong learning extends beyond gaining technical knowledge; it also includes understanding human behaviour and social dynamics.

Leaders who are committed to learning about others and the world can develop stronger empathy, which is vital for effective communication and team building. This understanding helps in nurturing a more inclusive and supportive workplace culture. More about these topics further in this book.

- **Personal and organizational growth:** Leaders who model learning behaviours inspire their teams to pursue knowledge and growth themselves. This can lead to higher levels of engagement and motivation within the team, as members feel supported in their own pursuits and see firsthand the value of continuous improvement. A learning culture within the organization can lead to overall organizational growth and success.

In essence, curiosity and lifelong learning enrich a leader's effectiveness and are instrumental in cultivating an environment where innovation, adaptability, and productivity thrive. These qualities ensure leaders not only manage the present well but are also well-prepared for the future. To stimulate your curiosity, you could embrace 'shoshin', a concept from Japanese Zen Buddhism meaning 'beginner's mind'. It refers to the idea of approaching life with an open and eager mind without preconceptions, just as a beginner would. This concept encourages curiosity, humility, and a willingness to learn and embrace new experiences, even in areas where one might already have significant expertise. It's about maintaining a fresh, open attitude in all endeavours, allowing for greater creativity and receptiveness to new possibilities. Whether you are ready to practise your 'shoshin' side or not, I can assure you that being curious is also fun. Daring to ask 'stupid' questions will open doors and bring insights beyond your imagination.

I had a fun learning experience as a result of curiosity. I travelled to Morocco with my daughter during Ramadan, the Islamic holy month of fasting. One evening we were hungry and came across a restaurant where the 'iftar' had just started. Iftar is the meal eaten by Muslims after sunset during Ramadan. The place was packed with locals – no tourists like us – and when the waiter asked us, in a friendly manner, to join the iftar buffet, we hesitated for a second. But the atmosphere was so welcoming that we joined this Muslim community to taste a delicious buffet. We not only ate great food, but we also learned more about how the fast is broken with the eating of dates. We spent a magnificent evening with delicious food and beverages, music, dancing and singing and when I asked my daughter her top three of our Moroccan holiday, the iftar was her best experience during this trip.

Enough about fun facts of travelling; let's talk about how a results-oriented focus can bring you more than time-controlled management.

STEP 7: RESULTS

When I interviewed entrepreneur and founder of Protime Peter s'Jongers[57] in my podcast, he vividly explained the benefits of time registration, the core activity of his company. He explained how time registration should be used like a smartwatch that measures your heartbeat while running. When you see your heart beating too fast, you should run slower to give your body the opportunity to recover and to avoid serious health risks. If you register that your people are working too many hours, you should intervene, hire more people, or redistribute tasks to others. It is a tool to prevent burnout and working too hard. Peter is smart enough to understand that his software tool to measure the amount of time people spend at their jobs is often abused to control the workforce. I wish more entrepreneurs and managers would use time registration like him! Peter has also written a super interesting book on company culture and new organizational structures. Listen to this interview in Dutch on your favourite audio podcast or watch it on my YouTube[58] channel with subtitles.

It has been scientifically proven that talent today wants to be judged on results, not on the number of hours they have spent on a task. The shift towards focusing on results rather than time management in leadership has garnered significant support based on various studies and expert opinions. This approach aligns with modern workplace trends that emphasise flexibility and productivity, recognising that rigid adherence to schedules does not necessarily equate to better outcomes. Diverse research highlights the effectiveness of results-focused leadership, suggesting that it not only enhances productivity but also fosters greater employee satisfaction. A balanced leadership approach that equally prioritises results and people has been found to be most effective. According to a survey cited by Perspectives LLC,[59] leaders who manage to balance a focus on results with attention to people's needs are perceived as great leaders by their employees 72% of the time.

One of the reasons many leaders still ask their staff back to the office is to watch them work. In-office work allows for easier monitoring of employee activities and many leaders still believe that if they watch people work, they work. Counting hours and watching people sit behind their desk or in meeting rooms might give you the perception of productivity, but it is not necessarily real productivity. Most people's productivity peaks under a set of optimised conditions that cater to both the organizational needs and individual employee preferences:

- **Giving them clear goals and objectives:** People are more productive when they understand what is expected of them. A simple rule, often forgotten.
- **Being a supportive leader:** A work environment that supports both physical and psychological well-being boosts productivity.
- **Let them work:** Allowing people a high degree of autonomy in how they accomplish their tasks can lead to higher job satisfaction and increased productivity. People tend to work more effectively when they can use their skills and organise their work in ways that they find most efficient. Reducing distractions in the workplace, whether they're physical distractions like noise or operational distractions like excessive meetings helps employees focus better and accomplish more.

Give it a try and trust your talent to handle their job without you watching closely. In most cases, they won't let you down!

STEP 8: STRATEGY

Strategy is my job! It has been my bread and butter since 2011 when I decided to leave a great job in a great advertising agency. Strategy is what keeps me going. My clients know that they can wake me up in the middle of the night if they have a strategic issue, a problem they are stuck with, new product development to help them grow, or a long-term goal they want to realise. But I need to be honest; the role of strategy and the need to have a long-term plan has changed dramatically. Today we live in a poly-crisis, meaning that we face simultaneous global challenges like pandemics, wars, economic inflation, climate change, energy shortages, and political instabilities. This term suggests that these crises are interconnected, and their combined impact is significant and complex. Covid made us all aware that things can suddenly be completely shaken up by external factors.

The Covid crisis was a turning point in my own career as a strategic consultant, as I had little work and plenty of time to research, which lead to the development of the CARE Principles framework. But it also helped me realise that making long-term strategies and defining a point in the far horizon as the goal to which the corporate ship sails is no longer possible in this VUCA (Volatility, Uncertainty, Complexity and Ambiguity) world. Strategy definitely remains important. You need to set long-term goals; it is great to define an engaging ambition and I love a commitment in vision statements! But as Erik-Jan Mares explained in the podcast interview in the previous chapter: '*A long term strategy is all about defining a horizontal line in the far horizon. It is no longer a dot, but a large horizontal line that drives our organization and gives it direction. We know in which direction we are heading; we don't know exactly at what point we will end.*'

Creating your long-term strategy that will help to engage your teams, empower them, and give them the energy to go the extra mile remains necessary. However, you need to build agility and flexibility into your strategic thinking. How can you do that? Here are some tips for strategies that you can employ to balance the need for a clear, long-term direction with the necessity for adaptability:

- **Review the yearly strategic offsite:** Organising strategic offsites is great, and I am a big fan of them as it is a moment to reflect on your future. However, I prefer to have several strategic offsites during the year. Ideally you start with a two-day offsite to define the long-term strategy and short-term goals with the management team. You follow this up with quarterly strategic offsites of half a day. You organise these regular strategic offsites outside your offices, ideally in different cities, to be combined with a brief trend safari in these cities: how do people eat, shop, dress, move themselves? Society is changing at a rapid pace – quicker in cities compared to rural areas – so keeping up with the pace of cities can help you sharpen and adapt your strategic plans.
- **Scenario planning:** Develop multiple scenarios of how the future might unfold. This helps anticipate changes and adapt strategies quickly. Take time to regularly update those scenarios as new information becomes available, or as events evolve.
- **Decentralise decision-making:** Once your strategy is defined, hand it over to the people. They are often the closest to the market reality, and are confronted with new issues that pop up or feel the impact of competitor's strategic moves. They talk to the clients; they feel the heartbeat of the busi-

ness on the field. Empower teams by letting them make most decisions on how to realise your goals and strategic plans.
- **Cross-train your people:** The more people understand the job of their colleagues, the more they are empathetic and willing to adapt certain procedures to help them. Siemens, for instance, offers various rotational development programmes across its global operations, including leadership development tracks where employees work in different departments and even different countries. Other examples are supermarket brands, for instance, where any management function needs to work in the shop and at the cashier, to better understand the work done on the field. This is also done in smaller companies; at Caffenation, a coffee roaster and coffee bar brand, all staff starts as a barista and gets thorough training on coffee knowledge and barista skills, so they can always take over a bar function, even if they work in a management function.
- **Open up for technology:** Leverage technology to enhance agility. For instance, use data analytics to gain real-time insights and predictive capabilities. Invest in systems that support rapid scaling or adjustments.
- **Enhance communication:** Tools like natural language processing can help automate and improve communication within teams, ensuring information is clear and accessible. If you are not a fan of ChatGPT, you can use alternative apps like Claude,[60] which is specifically built for the work environment.
- **Culture eats strategy:** You know that saying: 'Culture eats strategy for breakfast?' Unfortunately, having written hundreds of strategic plans in my career, I have to admit that it is so true. You can have the best strategy on paper, you can define an amazing ambition and a really stunning vision with the management team on a fun and inspiring strategic offsite... When your employees are not eager to execute that strategy, when they decide consciously or unconsciously to block or sabotage the plan and changes in behaviour that the new strategy requires, you can bet money on it that the plan will remain nice words on paper. Nothing will happen with it. Your people will help you realise your new strategy. It is of crucial importance! The single and only winning ingredient in successful strategic implementation is the involvement of your teams in this strategic work! The more you involve your teams in the strategy, the more transparent you are in the plans, the more you are vulnerable to let them shoot at it and give feedback on it, the more they will be willing to implement it and make it a success.

Forget the days when you made wild plans during a strategic offsite then thought you could command your people to execute these plans without asking for their support and feedback on them. Be prepared for their reluctance to change. Be open-minded about the changes they suggest. Dare to show vulnerability and a flexible mindset to adapt your strategy according to their feedback. You need all the brain in the game, remember! But in return for their support, energy, and efforts to execute and implement your strategies, they ask you to consider their need for a balanced life, with more room for mental health, with more room for physical health. Especially younger generations no longer want to live to work, they want to work to live – a change in mindset and a different perspective on the importance of work in life. In this aspect, we also need to learn how to build in an agile and flexible mindset. Let's talk about the need for more mental resilience in a world that creates so much fear among many people.

So, movement is key, and responsiveness drives movement. Gone are the days when we could create business and strategic plans years ahead and expect them to be etched in stone. Yes, planning is a necessity, particularly for long-term vision, positioning, and innovation, but short-term agility and flexibility are just as important. Agile leadership with radical adaptability is necessary today. Once you get comfortable with constant change, you will grow, pivot, and adapt to your transformational path towards success. Good luck with it!

STEP 9: RESILIENCE

Let's be clear, not everyone in society is anxious and fearful of the future. Many people are also excited about the technological changes, the cultural shift, innovations, a great job, a nice promotion, and whatever else the future will bring. However, there is an elephant in the room that needs to be addressed and that is stress, mental resilience, and mental well-being.

It is a fact that many people are simply afraid of all the changes ahead of us, and this anxiety is one of the reasons for higher levels of stress monitored in society. Research[61] shows worrying statistics on stress levels at all ages. This problem is a global one. According to the World Health Organization[62] and stress research by the American Psychiatric Association's 2024 mental health poll:[63]

- 15% of working-age adults were estimated to have a mental disorder in 2019.
- Globally, an estimated 12 billion working days are lost every year to depression and anxiety at a cost of US$1 trillion per year in lost productivity.
- Approximately 5 million deaths worldwide are attributed to mood and anxiety disorders each year.
- In 2024, 43% of American adults said they feel more anxious than they did the previous year, up from 37% in 2023 and 32% in 2022. Adults are particularly anxious about current events (70%) – especially the economy (77%), the 2024 U.S. election (73%), and gun violence (69%).

Whether we recognise this or not, whether we experience it or not, worldwide statistics show that mental health is in decline, and this comes at a cost. Since 2023, many employers have mainly focused on business outcomes amid a challenging economic market. They often fail to consider the cost of poor mental health in the workplace. According to Gallup,[64] in a nutshell, the true costs of poor mental health are:

- Burnt out employees cost $3.400 out of every $10.000 in salary, because they are disengaged in their work. We're talking about high turnover and lower productivity as main signals.
- The replacement cost of the average worker[65] is expensive; it is measured at as high as a half to two times the annual salary.

It takes empathy and curiosity to understand why people are feeling stressed. But it is not only the job, of course, that creates mental issues. American Gen Z are more likely than older adults (50+) to say social connection has the biggest impact on their mental health. Our technology-heavy world absolutely leads to increased stress in people of all ages, and AI will only accelerate this. But it is not only technostress that is giving us anxiety; many companies are turning back their HR policies of flexible work. All over the globe, we read how employees are forced back to sit in offices for eight hours a day. For many people, mental balance and work-life balance in general was built up through Covid by prioritising sport or walks in between work. For many women, taking care of household jobs in between calls and tasks at home had become standard procedure. With being back in the office – sometimes full-time – this newly found balance is gone.

Whatever the reason for the lack of mental resilience we witness in society today, it is like a persistent cancer that eats organizations from within. A staggering 62%[66] of people say they feel the weight of burnout. Next to this astounding number, having poor mental resilience has a horrible effect on the remaining employees who are often expected to do the work of those on sick leave. This trickles down negatively, increasing the workload on your mentally strongest teams, it waters down your culture, and it can create value conflicts. A second elephant in the room that needs to be addressed is the mental resilience of younger generations. As said before, older generations have been raised to work hard, play hard, to show resilience and to never give up. When these people are confronted with younger generations who face difficulties, who can't cope with stress, and are burdened by anxiety, their first reaction is often one of asking them to 'toughen up' or to 'grit your teeth'. Often this type of advice comes from a good intention to ask others to endure and persevere through hardship. However, in most cases this well-meant advice won't work.

A World Health Organization[67] report from 2021 states:
- Globally, one in seven 10–19-year-olds experiences a mental disorder, accounting for 13% of the global burden of disease in this age group.
- Depression, anxiety, and behavioural disorders are among the leading causes of illness and disability among adolescents.
- Suicide is the fourth leading cause of death among 15–29-year-olds.
- The consequences of failing to address adolescent mental health conditions extend to adulthood, impairing both physical and mental health and limiting their opportunities to lead fulfilling lives as adults.

Levels of anxiety among younger generations like Millennials and Gen Z are sky high. A 2023 Deloitte global study on Gen Z and Millennials shows staggering insights on why these generations feel stressed and work has a serious impact on them:
- Finances and the welfare of their families are the top stress drivers for both generations.
- 79% of Gen Z and 73% of Millennials are concerned about their own mental health.
- A number of factors contributing to stress levels are directly work-related for 60% of these respondents: heavy workload, poor work/life balance, un-

healthy team cultures, and inability to be their authentic self at work.
- They also struggle to disconnect from work, with 23% of Gen Zs and 30% of Millennials saying that they answer work email outside of business hours at least five days a week.
- Statista[68] reveals that 66% of the global Gen Z generation feel stress, 27% feel depressed. 64% of Millennials globally feel stress and 24% signal signs of depression.

Asking Gen Z to grit their teeth won't do the trick, as the reasons for their poor mental health are complex. Complaining that younger generations don't want to work like you did is also a losing strategy. Believe me, today it is a deeply rooted problem in teams. I have monthly conversations with leaders who believe that by complaining, shaming, controlling, and commanding younger generations they will adapt and change the way they want to work. No, the most talented won't adapt! They will either leave your organization and look for a more understanding boss, or they will keep their efforts to a bare minimum and have no engagement, no commitment to you. You cannot fight cultural and societal trends; they always change and if there is one thing that we know for sure, it is that humanity is always adapting itself.

A law and a different type of leadership is surely not the only solution to help this generation deal with the world as it is. Here are some tips to build and strengthen the mental resilience of all your people, independently of their age. Building mental resilience in your workforce is essential for enhancing job satisfaction, productivity, and overall well-being. Quality downtime is vital to overall productivity and well-being. Workers need opportunities – both in and out of the workplace – to reboot their internal systems and reclaim their creativity. Benefit schemes will be holistically re-imagined as workers demand more than gym memberships, in-office pool tables and after-work drinks. Both mental and physical well-being will be central to future employment packages. And overall, it will take courage and compassion to understand that younger generations chase different dreams than the ones we grew up with.

I meet talent directors who admit that their ambitious growth plans are jeopardised because they lose – on a yearly base – as many people as they hire, especially young talent. Many companies try to please them by organising after-work drinks or by installing fun work environments with table tennis tables etc. It no longer does the trick of keeping young generations engaged, as most don't want to attend after-work drinks, they want to go home and do stuff they choose to unwind, with the friends of their choice. Here are some effective strategies to address mental resilience for all generations, drawn from recent research and expert recommendations:

- **Stimulate a learning mindset**: Leaders can better cope with difficulties and lead their teams through challenging times with a positive outlook on learning skills and developing new things. Offering training and education in all kinds of soft and hard skills is a great way to take your own future into your hands. People who have that learning mindset are simply happier!

- **Establish a check-in culture:** Try to give continuous feedback and support. Regular check-ins not only help managers understand employees' challenges but also provide an opportunity to address these issues proactively. Often people are already helped with a listening ear, this alone can reduce stress and anxiety.

- **Encourage physical well-being:** You do not necessarily need to run marathons together, but companies that promote physical health do this because they know it positively impacts mental resilience. Promote activities that support physical health, such as regular exercise, adequate sleep, and a good work-life balance.

- **Make mental well-being a priority:** Talking openly and listening to your people about their issues with work pressure, stress, and anxiety are already great steps to allow people to let off steam. Offering coaching, whether through apps like Better Up[69] or Ezra[70] can help your people manage conflicts or simply understand their pitfalls. If you prefer live coaching, you can of course hire coaches that come to your office. An in between solution is offered from organizations such as Thrive Partners[71] in the U.K. They offer coaches from all over the world the possibility to coach through their platform, so employees can access a coach 24/7 in the language, at the hour and day of choice. Ideal for generations who like to work anytime, from anywhere, and address their worries instantly.

- **Promote healthy food:** There is adequate proof today of how food impacts our health and overall mood. You are what you eat is a compelling documentary on Netflix[72] about Stanford research on the impact of food tested on identical twins. The study found that, after only eight weeks, the twins eating the plant-based diet experienced: an increase in their life expectancy; reduced visceral fat (the dangerous fat that accumulates around your organs); reduced risk of heart disease; and even heightened sexual drive. The results surprised even the Stanford research team. I had the pleasure to work with a big catering company who teamed up with a chef specialised in sports nutrition. Together we developed a future-proof healthy catering strategy for corporates. This chef experienced how certain food heals injuries faster, and specific diets have a boosting effect on the mindset of sportspeople. So, plenty of proof to ask your caterer to review your food offering to make it more sustainable, healthier and with a positive impact on brain power!

- **Invest in social connections:** A robust social support network at work can buffer stress and enhance resilience. Encourage team-building activities and mentorship programmes to strengthen these bonds. I am not a big fan of the obliged move to being back in the office, but to monitor the well-being of your team and to foster the culture, it is good to see each other on a regular basis. Discuss openly with your team what works best for them and involve them in the policies you make around this topic.

- **Privilege is invisible to those who have it:** I talked about this before, and in the next topic I explain who opened my eyes to that, but in terms of mental resilience it also helps to accept that we all have different levels of resilience. Saying you don't get stressed out by X or Z does not help those who do feel stress. Acknowledging their feelings is really a great first step. The home situation also impacts how we feel at work. We don't leave behind our private worries when we enter the company, we do not always know what is going on in the lives of people if they choose not to mention it. So, embrace your kind and caring side and dare to show compassion. This approach helps individuals recover from setbacks more quickly and fosters a positive work environment.

- **Be open about failure:** Curiosity helps to view failures and setbacks as opportunities to learn, which is key to building resilience. Small events or group sessions like Fuck-up Fridays help to create an open culture in which people share their failures, their mistakes, their fuck-ups. Organizations like 'Fuckup Nights'[73] help to remove the stigma of failure. Openness to making mistakes and not being punished for things that go wrong are surely helping people to keep their courage and willingness to crawl back up after falling.

- **Monitor and protect your people:** Track the workload and intervene when you see that people start to have too much work. A new project, a burnt-out colleague, a change in the team structure – often invisible and tiny things start a chain of stress and mental overload. With good measuring tools, but also with a simple question like 'How are you feeling today?' you can prevent rather than cure.

I understand today's reality on the work floor is complex and complicated. Being confronted with generations who share their mental issues in TikTok videos creates resistance among many leaders; quiet (and loud) quitting, bore- and burnouts – what else do you need to consider? Well, to remain agile and up to speed with society, it is more than time to embrace diversity and inclusion, step number 10 in the leadership model.

STEP 10: DIVERSITY & INCLUSION

The roots of modern diversity and inclusion initiatives can be traced back to the civil rights movement in the United States during the 1960s, which prompted legislative changes such as the Civil Rights Act of 1964. This act was crucial in addressing racial discrimination and was later expanded to include gender, ethnicity, and other forms of discrimination. During the 1970s and 1980s, the focus expanded to include affirmative action, which aimed to address the inequalities in employment and education opportunities for minorities and women. You would think we had made progress since the sixties. The reality is that today among the top 100 American companies, women hold only 9% of CEO positions.[74] In Europe, we are not doing better; only 7.8% of CEO positions among the largest publicly listed companies in the European Union are held by female leaders.

Diversity and inclusion are seen as critical elements of corporate strategy linked to performance and innovation. We see a lot of talk about it; less action, unfortunately. When we look at the C-level in most organizations, there are still mainly men, white people, and most of them of 40+ in age. Many companies have managed to attract younger people, or people of colour, but it is still rare to see them take a place at the management table.

Diversity can be thought of as being invited to a party, while inclusion means being asked to dance when you're at the party. It's about actively engaging everyone in activities, ensuring they feel welcomed and valued, not just present. Diversity and inclusion are such vast topics with so many aspects that it is impossible to cover them all.

A key dimension in inclusion is identity for the next generations. Generalisations and objectifications of gender, race, sexuality, and ethnicity are no longer accepted. We have come to a point in history at which we have learnt from and undone the wrongs of the past – exemplified by cancel culture. Universities are implementing 'safe-zones' – spaces where students are safe from judgmental stereotypes and preconceptions over sexuality, biological gender, cultural ethnicity, or neurologic conformity. Will safe zones become expected in our workspaces too? We don't know, but we believe that the next generations are cared for more by schools and universities and this care will be demanded by them in their jobs too.

Granted, it is a difficult debate and especially on the work floor it is not always easy to cater for the level of personalisation and individualisation that people expect today. Here again we seem to be in a liquid state of transformation, not sure what the new normal will look like. I was very happy that I could exchange ideas and learn from my conversation with Hanan Challouki, founder of Inclusified. In the podcast that you can listen to below, we talk extensively of the need for more diversity on the work floor, and how this will change leadership and talent management tomorrow. Her experience on making cultures more inclusive for more diverse people is crucial. However, in this step towards a more agile organization, I want to talk about the feeling of inclusivity: the feeling that you belong. The feeling that you matter, despite differences in age, gender, sexual orientation, neurodiversity, disability, race, ethnicity, religion, or cultural background. There is no room here to dive into all these aspects, but I will highlight a few – the ones closest to my heart!

■ Gender

In 2017, I found myself immersed in the Fast Company Innovation Festival[75] in New York, surrounded by the buzz of keynotes, debates, and engaging talks. One discussion that left a lasting impression focused on diversity and inclusion. A retired American sociologist[76] – who specialised in gender studies – suggested that 'privilege is invisible to those who have it'. He emphasised the need for a broader understanding of gender beyond women and highlighted a compelling trend – men often become instant feminists when they become fathers to daughters. Research[77] indicated that male CEOs with daughters were more inclined to lead socially responsible firms. Daughters can influence their fathers even from infancy! The Danish minister of culture Jakob Engel-Schmidt was inspired by his newborn baby daughter to question the gender of statues in Copenhagen.[78] Less than 10% of statues in the city are female, so he decided to reserve 6 million euros to rectify this gender imbalance.

This revelation struck a personal chord, as I have two beautiful daughters, but it also resonated with the experience of Olivier Van Cauwelaert, sustainable and social entrepreneurship catalyst. In the CARE Principles podcast,[79] he humorously reflected on his shift from luxury cars to impactful, sustainable entrepreneurship, all catalysed by his daughters urging him to embrace responsibility, and work for impact and not fancy cars. He thoroughly changed his lifestyle and job, and today he is one of the most future-oriented, radical eco-minded entrepreneurs. Not all CEOs I have met since have made such a radical choice as Olivier, but I have come across several male leaders who woke up to the bias they had towards women and who embraced the CARE Principles, simply because their daughters had warmed them up towards a leadership style that is more caring, sustainable, inclusive, empathetic, and focused on collaboration and trust.

As a woman and a mother, this heartening phenomenon aligns with my belief that the much-needed transformation in leadership will be propelled by those who embrace a softer, kinder version of themselves – irrespective of gender. CARE Leadership is about embracing your female traits, even as a male leader. I am also happy to witness a new generation of female leaders who have no problem showing their caring side, while being a top-notch successful executive! Male and female leaders who have impressive careers while prioritising childcare are leaving the office at 4 p.m. There is surely a shift happening for the better, and we are just at the start of this revolution.

The gender gap remains a serious issue despite all the awareness that doesn't seem to have any effect on reality. The gender pay gap in Belgium – meaning the difference in hourly wages between women and men – amounts to 5%. This means that in 2022, Belgian women earned on average 5% less than their male colleagues for the same job. The European statistics are even worse, at 12,7%, and some American numbers run up to an 18% pay gap.[80] Whatever statistic you consider, the fact is that the pay gap persists even though women today are more likely than men to graduate from college and university. In fact, the pay gap between college-educated women and men is not any narrower than the one between women and men who do *not* have a college degree. This points to the dominant role of various factors that still set women back. Parenthood is still the biggest reason why women stop working or start to work part-time, giving them serious career interruptions and reducing their experience. Even when women want to continue to work full-time after the birth of their children, societal expectations often push back too.

My daughter was born in Amsterdam as I lived there at the time. It was simply impossible to find childcare for five days a week. I also underestimated the negative reactions – often from other women – when they found out I preferred to work full-time, instead of part-time. Even today Dutch society looks down on women who work full-time and with the high cost of childcare, many women still choose a part-time career. But working mums are not only condemned by society. A successful female lawyer felt that she was given fewer opportunities during her first pregnancy, even though pregnancy did not hold her back. After her second maternity leave, the management team led her to understand that becoming a partner at the law firm was no longer an option. They suggested that she choose for her kids. A suggestion that nobody would make to a young dad, right? So, the bias against women in the C-suite and the pay gap remains an aspect we need to keep on the business agenda.

> **My biggest failure ever is that I have failed to empower my feminine traits. To become a successful executive, I had to empower my masculine side, until I realised that true leaders don't do.**
>
> **We be.**
>
> **Being is what the feminine traits are about. We are not able to nourish and care in a society driven by masculinity. We should empower females and not force them into our game of masculinity. The world needs to wake up to that.**
>
> **It is my biggest failure and that of our society.**
>
> **MO GAWDAT, FORMER CHIEF BUSINESS OFFICER AT GOOGLE X**

But diversity is of course about more than just gender.

■ **Sexual orientation**

Writing and researching this book has also made me understand how biased I am on many levels, even though I consider myself open-minded, curious, and inclusive. For instance, I am a huge believer in LGTBQI+, but I must think deeply about what it stands for and how to act on it in leadership. LGBTQI+ stands for Lesbian, Gay, Bisexual, Transgender, Queer or Questioning, and Intersex, with the '+' representing other sexual identities, orientations, and communities.

This acronym is used to describe a diverse group of individuals who differ from the heterosexual and cisgender norm due to their sexual orientation, gender identity, or gender expression. Earlier in my career, I mostly worked in liberal and creative environments in which it was not a problem to openly say you were gay or lesbian, but I realise that that is not the case in all work environments, nor all countries.

I lived in Amsterdam before and today I live in Antwerp, two very open-minded and tolerant cities for people with different sexual orientation. Last year I was almost in tears when I watched the Gay Pride[81] parade as it was opened by the police team who proudly participated as members of the LGBTQI+ community. When a hard professional and male-oriented environment like the police force participates in Gay Pride, you know you live in a tolerant city! Another experience I can recommend all curious and open-minded people to go to watch is the 'Vogue Ball bootcamps', something I discovered in the Singel,[82] the Antwerp arts centre with a great and diverse programming.

'Vogue Ball' or simply 'ball' are events where participants from the LGBTQ+ community, particularly those who are Black and Latinx, come together to compete in dance, fashion, and performance categories. This scene originated in New York City in the eighties. I got to know this through a series on Netflix called Pose.[83] It is a fictional series but based on the 'ball houses' that emerged in New York. 'Voguing' is a highly stylised form of dance that originated from these balls, characterised by model-like poses inspired by Vogue magazine, combined with angular, linear, and rigid arm, leg, and body movements. Madonna made this vogue style famous.

The community that dances at these balls provides support, camaraderie, and a safe space for self-expression, especially for those who may feel marginalised elsewhere in society. It's a celebration of identity, resilience, and creativity, offering an important cultural outlet for many in the LGBTQ+ community.

Some organizations like Google offer comprehensive transgender-inclusive healthcare benefits, and have policies in place to support transitioning employees, including guidelines around using preferred names/pronouns and access to gender-neutral restrooms. If you want to embrace inclusion for this community, be sure to be authentic about it, as the LGBTQ+ community is calling out corporations like Anheuser-Busch over its poor handling of the conservative backlash their Bud Light campaign got with the transgender influencer Dylan Mulvaney.[84] Human Rights associations took them to court and today the brand is back to conservative sport sponsorships. The popular quote 'There is no such thing as bad advertising' might need an update as this brewer has lost billions in market value over this brief partnership with Mulvaney and then backing out of it under influence of their conservative consumer base.[85] It keeps on surprising me how huge brands like Bud Light or Pepsi make non-conscious and inauthentic choices again and again. What you stand for and, particularly in the States, which political side you take became an issue of utter importance. Your fan base will no longer accept any opportunistic actions if they are not grounded deeply into your brand. Enough about culture, marketing, and branding; what is showing leadership for people with a different sexual orientation? I guess here it also boils down to being curious, open-minded, authentic, daring to ask the stupid questions, and being non-judgmental about it.

■ **Ageism**

An aspect I hear a lot about – probably because I am not a junior myself anymore – is age discrimination at work. Despite great initiatives like the Foodbag brand who hire retired people as drivers to deliver their meal boxes, kicking out people of a certain age is still a widely spread practice. The impact of age discrimination is felt across all company sizes and is not confined to specific sectors. SHRM[86] reported that age discrimination is not only widespread but also manifests in various forms including biased job advertisements, derogatory comments, and unfair employment practices such as pressured resignations or unfair dismissals often disguised as layoffs. Studies also show that age discrimination can start relatively early in an individual's career, with many experiencing it as early as their forties.

This form of discrimination not only affects the morale and productivity of older employees but can also lead to significant financial and emotional stress. The persistence of ageism highlights the need for continued advocacy and the implementation of strict anti-discrimination laws and policies within companies to protect older workers and ensure a fair and inclusive working environment. It is such a pity because the older generations can be of such value to organizations. Not only because of their knowledge and experience but, as mentioned before, the best way to avoid bias in an organization is to have a large representation of society. I agree that laws and regulations are not always helpful. I met brilliant and driven professors who were obliged to leave university at the age of 65. I met highly successful salespeople who were forced into retirement by laws, I met dedicated female executives of 50 who were neglected and brought close to burnout by young managers. All people still of high value to their organizations and society at large, all forced into lesser pay, retirement, sick leave, and loss of self-esteem.

For most people, a job is a reason to get out of bed, to serve society, to have a meaning and to be actively part of society. Not everyone is keen on having more free time, or filling days with voluntary work. A fundamental discussion about the role of elderly people in society needs to take place, but it is too large a discussion to be held here. I can only ask you to think twice before laying off people of age, especially those with drive, and craving to help your organization thrive. Create an inclusive culture in which everyone feels at ease. But with so many aspects and traits of people to deal with, it often feels like a minefield.

PODCAST INTERVIEW

WITH HANAN CHALLOUKI, FOUNDER OF INCLUSIFIED AND HIJABS AT WORK

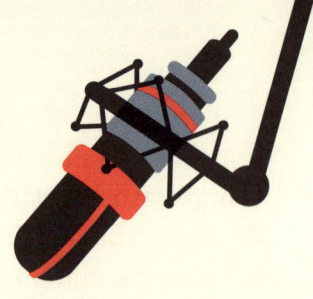

Hanan Challouki is an influential entrepreneur and diversity champion, with a profound dedication to fostering inclusivity and representation, Hanan has emerged as a leading voice in promoting diversity within professional environments. Through Inclusified, she provides strategic guidance to organizations aiming to create more inclusive workplaces, ensuring that diversity is not just a policy but a lived reality. Additionally, her initiative, Hijabs at Work, empowers veiled Muslim women to navigate and thrive in their careers while embracing their identities. Hanan's work bridges cultural gaps and paves the way for a more equitable society, making her a pivotal figure in the movement towards greater inclusion and representation in the workplace. Her visionary leadership and tireless advocacy have garnered widespread recognition, and I was happy that she took the time to share her thoughts on the CARE Principles podcast.

> **Superdiversity is not going anywhere. This is what we're living right now. And it's only going to be more and more, we're never going back.**
>
> **HANAN CHALLOUKI, INCLUSIVE STRATEGIST**

Hanan's leadership tips:
- TIP 1: For organizations that still need to start with DEI, have an idea of where you are right now when it comes to diversity, equity and inclusion. Many people can't really reply to that question. They have a gut feeling but no real data.
- TIP 2: For those who want to, like, really go faster, I would suggest starting with the leaders. Inclusive leadership is one of the most important things when it comes to creating change in the DEI field. Because people look at the leaders, people see them as role models. If they carry out inclusive values, it will be a lot easier to create a support base and to have other people do the same as well.

Spotify link to podcast episode

https://spotifyanchor-web.app.link/e/fDurKBBtgMb

AGILITY EXERCISES

Curiosity: YES DAY

Solo exercise
Install a 'yes' day at the office for each team member, including yourself if you are the boss. The idea of this exercise is that you reply 'yes' to all questions that you are asked. Questions from your team, but also questions from external team members. Note: you can use one wildcard if there is a really a question that could potentially create damage to you or your organization. Be aware that the team members cannot know who has the 'yes day', as it must happen as spontaneously as possible.

Purpose of the exercise: To feel what happens when you affirm a choice or action you would normally say 'no' to. Does this change the course of some decisions? Does it create a different energy? Does it open doors and lead to breakthrough thinking?

Results: THE MARSHMALLOW CHALLENGE[87]

Team-building exercise
This is an exercise for when you have time, so it's ideal on a team-building event. It demonstrates the value of focusing on results and innovation over time spent and promotes the idea of creative thinking and effectiveness.

Materials needed:
- 20 sticks of uncooked spaghetti
- 1 roll of masking tape
- 1 meter of string
- 1 marshmallow
- A timer (to keep track, but not to pressure)

Group size: 4–5 people per team
Duration: 18 minutes
Instructions. Set up: Divide participants into small teams of 4–5 people.

Give each team the same materials: 20 sticks of spaghetti, 1 meter of string, 1 roll of masking tape, and 1 marshmallow.

Challenge: Each team has 18 minutes to build the tallest free-standing structure that supports the marshmallow at the top using only the provided materials. The marshmallow needs to be at the top, and the structure must stand on its own. Emphasise that the result (height and stability of the structure) is what counts, not how much time they spend planning versus building. After the timer goes off, measure each structure. Discuss which teams were successful and why.

Purpose of this exercise: This is the most important element of this fun exercise!
- Ask teams to reflect on how they used their time and how focusing solely on time might have impacted their creativity or final product.
- Lead a discussion on how this activity can relate to workplace projects. Highlight the importance of focusing on the quality and innovativeness of the outcome rather than the amount of time spent. Discuss how creativity can be stifled when employees are constantly watching the clock.

Strategy: SCENARIO PREP

Team exercise
The objective of this team exercise is to enhance quick thinking and rapid decision-making skills in unexpected corporate scenarios.

Duration: 30 minutes

Materials needed:
- Pen and paper or a digital device for note taking
- Timer
- Scenario cards (prepared beforehand, see below for examples)

Preparation:
Create scenario cards: Write down different unexpected corporate scenarios on individual cards. Examples include:

1. 'Your largest client just announced they are switching to a competitor.'
2. 'A sudden power outage affects the entire office for the day.'
3. 'An important project deadline is moved up by two weeks.'
4. 'A social media post from your company goes viral for the wrong reasons.'
5. 'A key supplier unexpectedly goes out of business.'

The team takes one scenario from the bowl and individually starts to write down a rapid response plan (five minutes).

Each participant takes two minutes to present their scenario and response plan. After each presentation, the other participants have a moment to provide feedback and suggest improvements.

Discuss what was learned from the exercise. Clarify how each participant can play a different role in vision/skills/tools they can bring to the table.

Reflect on the effectiveness of the rapid responses and feedback provided.

Identify quick tips for improving rapid decision-making in future unexpected situations.

Purpose of this exercise: To allow teams to practise and improve their ability to quickly develop and articulate effective strategies for handling unexpected situations, all within a short timeframe.

Diversity & Inclusion: CONNECT INSTEAD OF REJECT

Solo exercise
Objective of the exercise: To recognise your judgments and then do something different from what you are used to doing (bias). This way, you can experience the power of diversity and inclusion.

You are walking down the street or going to the supermarket.

Become aware of all the people around you, especially those who look different from you.

Notice what happens in your body and mind (thoughts) when you see someone you have a judgment about, for whatever reason. (A judgment is not something you 'do'; it happens unconsciously).

Once you have a certain judgment, notice the urge you get. Do you want to turn your head away, walk quickly, or leave?

The invitation now is to do something different: Smile at the person or say hello or give a compliment or start a conversation.

What do you see happening with the other person when you do that? And what does that do to you?

What changes when you don't 'move away' from what is different, but instead move towards it?

Beyond your biases – beyond what you know and are used to.

NOTE:
Also apply this exercise if there is a hiring process going on in the organization. Notice how we automatically tend to hire people who are like us – people who look or behave in ways we are accustomed to. Challenge yourself to reach beyond that. Practise embracing diversity and experience its power.

Purpose of this exercise: To remove biases we all have. To look at people who differ from you in race, ethnicity, gender, gender identity, sexual orientation, age, disability, socio-economic-cultural background, religion… without fear or judgment.

Resilience: CHANGE PERSPECTIVES

Team exercise
Define together a recent problem that has occurred in the organization.

Each member of the team gives his perspective of the problem, in 1 minute max.

Be silent for 2 minutes then write down your answer to: what is the greater gift of this issue?

What did you learn from this problem?

What is the opportunity of this situation and what breakthrough here might be possible to learn from?

Each member reads his new perspective on the problem aloud out to the others.

Purpose of this exercise: to learn how to look from different perspectives and angles to a problem and to learn how to turn a problem into an opportunity. Don't wait as a victim and stay stuck in this situation; show creativity and resilience and solution-based thinking to come out of this issue stronger.

**Can't wait to read about
RELIABILITY?**

PLAY SECTION 7
RELIABILITY IS ESSENTIAL

Being a respectful, trustworthy organization that values integrity and honesty is probably something that all companies believe in. On the list of values most companies develop, integrity is nearly always mentioned. Unfortunately, corporate whistleblower reports reveal cases of toxic leadership, fraud, misleading and/or unethical behaviour. With a society in rapid transformation, pushed by technology, people look at their leaders to make the right, conscious and ethical choices. More than ever, reliability is linked with authenticity and the open and transparent reasons behind certain choices. The choices that are made can divide employees, can create a 'divide and conquer' culture that leads to a mentality of 'them' against 'us'. This can go so far that it can make the organization implode, especially when laws are broken because a part of the organization has lost track of reality. I have experienced this up close: a case in which the CEO ended up in jail. More about this staggering leadership failure in the culture part: step three of the five steps on how to build a reliable reputation with culture.

The Edelman Trust Barometer[88] states that 92% of employees expect their CEO to speak out about societal challenges. CEOs should take the lead and be seen as agents of change in society. They could become the rock stars of tomorrow, and their reliability score and trustworthiness will give them more power than their economic value. They will not only lead their enterprise; they will also represent the loudest voice from within the industry and show their stakeholders – and not just their shareholders – what they care about and how valuable it is to them. Business leaders all over the world have started to realise this. In the 'Decade to deliver' report from the UN and Accenture,[89] it's fascinating to read the number of CEOs who are aware that they can be part of the change needed and who want to contribute to the seventeen Global Goals set out in the report,[90] such as climate action, poverty reduction, gender equality, and so on. Of the CEOs that participated, 76% say citizen trust will be critical to business competitiveness in their industry in the next 5 years.

However, we see trust is in decline on a global level. In the latest Trust Barometer people from 28 countries state that:
- 61% of business leaders are purposely trying to mislead people by saying things they know are false or gross exaggerations.
- Especially when people look at innovations and the rapid social change, the reliability scores of CEOs (51%), journalists (47%) and government leaders (45%) is rapidly in decline. People give similar trust to scientists and people like them (both score 74%).
- People not only fear losing their jobs to innovations, or AI, but fear inflation, climate change, hackers, nuclear war, and the disinformation war.

Leaders need to choose on which side of history they want to stand. Until they do, let's have a look at the most common blocks to building your reputation.

RELIABILITY HURDLES

There was a time when reliability mainly applied to the factual aspects of a company: offering a reliable product, having a good reputation with your clients, scoring high in the ranks of best employer lists, having trustworthiness as one of your company values. All these things build your company's reliability factor. For decades now, trust has been built through marketing. Creating a decent product, adding a robust brand identity, showcasing it through a trustworthy brand image and using storytelling to enhance your great achievements.

It is important to understand that building a reputation today is not done like in the old days. For decades, trust was built through marketing and advertising. Trust was basically built through carefully manicured actions, campaigns, and images. But let's face it, your brand image was often far from reality. That was okay. That was the way the whole world used to build a trustworthy brand image! We all participated in this picture-perfect life! That was how it was done in the past. Today we need to move on. Today the morality of brands and people are questioned, and trust is created through a different attitude. An attitude of more honesty, and more authenticity. But that is not the only reason why a reliable reputation has to be built in different ways.

An increase in technology, data, and connectivity results in audiences having higher expectations and lower attention spans when it comes to content. Audiences have a habit of checking social (83%), search (73%), and news sites and apps (77%) at least once or multiple times daily,[91] which means your company is no longer people's sole source of brand reliability. Your company exists in an exposed, public space, where people will dig into your brand on all levels. When your information is unreliable, despite your manicured employer branding campaigns, the truth will come out faster than you can imagine. We live in an era where politicians get away with lies, wars, toxic and harmful behaviour. We live in a society where media brands prefer clickbait to fact checking and copy-paste news without even trying to find out whether there is any truth to it.

In this digital world, many suffer from FOMO – the fear of missing out – and have split-second updates and constant streams of information on their screens. These streams of information are different for you than for me as we live in digital bubbles or reality tunnels, as the American psychologist Timothy Leary[92] and author Robert Wilson call them. We all individually create reality tunnels as a subconscious set of mental filters formed from beliefs and experiences. Through these tunnels, individuals interpret the same world differently. Algorithms feed these tunnels and push only messages that confirm our thinking and acting. Seeing the world through our own lenses, stimulated, and fed by (social) media algorithms, gives us a view on reality that might be very different from others' views. Many political parties' growth is based on feeding this polarisation, even with fake news. These algorithms can lead to polarisation in society, but also within organizations. I see leaders who have dug themselves so deep into their 'truth' about their team that there is no more willingness to understand them and connect with them. It can be dangerous when we feel less and less common ground, and room to understand others. Fear is often the psychological driver behind a fixed idea and conviction that your own truth is the only truth. That others are wrong and need to adapt their behaviour to meet yours. It takes diplomacy, time, and special tactics to work with leaders who have dug themselves into deep reality tunnels.

> **When we meet somebody whose separate tunnel-reality is obviously far different from ours, we are a bit frightened and always disoriented. Yet it is neurologically obvious that no 2 brains have the same genetically programmed hard wiring, the same imprints, the same conditioning, the same learning experiences. We are all living in separate realities. That is why communication fails so often, and misunderstandings and resentments are so common.**
>
> **ROBERT ANTON WILSON, NOVELIST**

We live in such transformational times that 69% of people[93] say that society is changing too quickly in ways that are not beneficial to them. People are concerned that science is losing its independence to governments, to politicians and to the wealthy. Despite the decline in global trust, there is also hope. Overall, the 2024 Edelman Trust Barometer finds that the most trusted institution remains business (63%). Businesses are far ahead of government based on perception of high competence (business scores 52 points higher) and ethics (business scores 32 points higher). Indeed, it is business that is most trusted in ensuring that the introduction of innovations is well managed (59%) and to manage change in our social values (57%).
But business leaders should not take public trust for granted. Business's trusted status in society is not a given, and without active management could go the same way as trust in government and media.

So, let's have a look at how to build trust, first and foremost among your teams, as trust and a good reputation starts within your inner circle. Trust is not built overnight and cannot be created in an executive meeting room. It is a bottom-up process that starts with receiving trust from your employees. It is an inside-out process that acts on many different levels towards all your stakeholders: your employees, your community, your customers, your suppliers, your vendors, your local government. Trust comes in many shapes and forms and will be linked to authenticity and transparency drivers. Trust is palpable in company cultures and values. Reliability is built through support and positivism.

ARE ORGANIZATIONS RELIABLE?

According to the CARE Scan they are! Though the benchmark study was done only in Belgium, it is still interesting to look at the data.

Figure 10: Care Scan reliability scores.

Reliability has the highest score in the benchmark study! Being a trustworthy partner for stakeholders gets a staggering 70/100 score, the highest of all scores! But internal reliability also scores well, at 64%. 23% of employees are convinced that their employer does not focus only on profit, but also pursues important social goals. 34% of employees somewhat agree with this statement; only 8% completely disagree. This means that many organizations show their heart for social issues. Also, the trust in management is high: 67% of employees believe their management is honest and reliable. 75% of them believe they receive a fair salary. 47% of employees have seen how their organization adapted their business model to place more emphasis on sustainability.

As mentioned before, the global research from the Edelman Trust Barometer confirms an overall belief of people in the reliability of businesses. Does this mean you can lean back and skip this chapter? Better not, as trust arrives on foot and leaves on horseback! Check out the five steps to remain or become a reliable leader!

THE 5 STEPS TO BE(COME) A RELIABLE LEADER

STEP 11: SAFETY

It is very simple here: When people do not feel safe, they cannot function well, and we are referring here to both safeties – physical and psychological. In the collaboration chapter, we talked a lot about trust and obviously it is related to this chapter, so this safety chapter will not be too long. But remember that safety is a foundation of human functioning. Psychological safety is a tricky one, because it can remain under the radar of the leadership team for a long time. A pity, as it is a crucial stepping-stone of giving and receiving trust. Psychological safety at work is crucial for effective team performance, innovation, and employee satisfaction. However, several factors can contribute to a lack of psychological safety in the workplace, making people feel insecure or uncomfortable about taking risks, asking questions, or expressing their opinions. Here are some important reasons why psychological safety may be compromised:

- **Fear on the work floor:** According to the Harvard Business Review, about 30% of the workforce are bullied at work.[94] In countries like India, that percentage can rise to 55%. In Germany statistics reveal lower numbers of 17%. Bullying receives little attention and action as it is often a complex issue. It is crucial to create safe work environments for all employees – regardless of their position. There are 15 features mapped to common archetypes of bullies. From the 'screamers' who yell and fist-bang to the quieter 'schemers' who use gaslighting techniques to push colleagues out. Whatever the type of bullying, as long as an organization allows it, it will continue. Training of all staff and addressing it immediately are effective methods to deal with this. Other fear issues are about being scared to make mistakes or that admitting failure could lead to negative consequences, such as criticism,

blame, or even job loss. This fear can discourage them from speaking up or trying new things.
- **Lack of support from the management:** When leaders do not actively support open communication and fail to encourage diverse opinions, employees may feel that their input is not valued or respected. Managers who do not model or enforce respectful behaviour can contribute to an unsafe environment.
- **Discrimination and bias:** Prejudice based on race, gender, age, or other personal characteristics can severely impact psychological safety. When employees face discrimination or bias, they are less likely to feel secure and supported in the workplace.
- **Highly competitive cultures:** In workplaces where competition is emphasised over collaboration, employees may feel pressured to outperform their colleagues at all costs, leading to cutthroat behaviour and a lack of trust among team members.
- **Poor and untransparent communication:** Ambiguities in roles, expectations, and processes can contribute to a lack of psychological safety. Without clear communication, employees may feel uncertain about their responsibilities and the appropriateness of their actions.
- **Lack of inclusion:** When employees are not included in decision-making processes or do not see transparency in how decisions are made, they may feel undervalued and powerless, reducing their sense of safety.

Creating a psychologically safe workplace involves addressing these issues directly through leadership training, clear communication, inclusive practices, transparency, fairness, ethical norms, and equitable and legitimate ways to obtain rewards. It requires a commitment from all levels of an organization to foster an environment where every employee feels safe to express themselves without fear of negative consequences.

Physical safety is also crucial and needs no extensive explanation. Protecting your employees from injuries, accidents, keeping safety procedures top of mind, and minimising health hazards seems standard procedure for most organizations. However, sometimes organizations are overly preoccupied with applying the safety instructions. A friend worked for a global manufacturing company with oil rigs. The company's safety instructions stated that employees had to hold onto stair railings when going up or down, which made sense on oil rigs and in construction plants with dangerous staircases. But he worked in the fancy, modern headquarters with normal office stairs. Nobody was allowed to walk up and down these stairs without holding firmly onto the stair railings! He received reprimands from colleagues when he walked down the middle of the staircase with his hands in his pockets, for instance. There had never been stair accidents in this HQ, yet everyone was drilled to apply the corporate safety rules, even when they made little sense. Anyway, the point about safety is that it is a crucial first step in becoming a reliable leader!

STEP 12: AUTHENTICITY

Is it not time to be open, transparent, honest, and authentic? Is it not time to dare to admit that perfection doesn't exist? Is it not time to admit that we are in the midst of a non-stop process of transformation, and that this process will always have a few blind spots somewhere? That's okay. Reliable leaders know that they don't know it all. They understand and accept that they have limitations too. After all, they are human. The best leaders hire people smarter and more capable than them. They have no issues with publicly admitting what they don't understand and from whom they want help.

The important lesson about reliability is not to try to cover up your shortcomings. Talk about them openly and sincerely. The famous British entrepreneur Richard Branson, who created the Virgin Group, openly discusses his struggles with dyslexia, a learning disorder characterised by difficulties with reading, spelling, and writing. He has no shame in admitting that he doesn't know how to read an accounting balance sheet. Still, he owns hundreds of companies across various industries, including music, airlines, telecommunications, and health services, and he is considered to be a very charismatic and authentic leader.

Being yourself is so much easier and less stressful than trying to pretend or trying to fit into a straitjacket that prevents you from being your true, authentic self. But remaining true to oneself is not always that easy, because we are often burdened by expectations from others. For instance, in our private lives, our parents expect something different from us. But of course, the pressure to align with corporate culture, cultural habits or simply mentions of 'that is how we do it here' push many people away from who they are at the core. It is a fine balancing act to continue to learn, evolve, and grow as person, while remaining true and close to oneself. It is a steep learning curve to allow introspection and discover what you really want. You, not others. It takes honesty and courage to look yourself in the mirror and accept yourself with all your flaws and shortcomings. But when you do, you are unbeatable! People feel that in their gut, and trust authentic leaders more for a couple of reasons:

- **Consistency:** Authentic leaders demonstrate consistency between their words and actions. When leaders act in ways that align with their stated values and beliefs, it reinforces trust among their followers.
- **Integrity:** They uphold high ethical standards, value honesty, and stick to their Principles, which earns them respect and trust from others. Showing their true selves – including their vulnerabilities – makes them more relatable and approachable.
- **Respect:** They value diverse opinions and encourage open communication. By respecting and valuing the contributions of others, authentic leaders foster an environment of trust.
- **Inspirational:** They often have a clear vision and passion that inspire others. Their genuine enthusiasm and commitment can motivate teams, leading to greater trust and engagement.
- **Empathy:** As seen in the next play section, authentic leaders demonstrate genuine concern for the well-being of their employees. They listen actively and respond to their team's needs, which builds emotional bonds and trust.

But as I said before, it is not so easy to stay true to yourself. If you are not a moral fighter, nor someone who has the ability to trust your gut, that is okay. If you have difficulty finding your state of flow, that is a pity, but it is not insurmountable. If you have never really thought about your inner compass and intuition or you are simply a person without strong opinions on that level and you maintain your integrity without having them clearly written out, that is perfect. What is important in life is to align your actions with your values and beliefs. This is crucial for a happy, balanced personal identity and your self-respect. Staying close to yourself builds resilience and feels natural. You could say that when you are your authentic self you are in a natural state of flow, like when you were a kid.

But understanding who you truly are, and finding your authentic self is often a journey on its own. I did several things that were not really aligned with myself; I engaged with people whose values were quite the opposite of mine, ignoring my inner voice and chasing their dreams instead of mine. With age and experience, with pain and disappointment, and with introspection and compassion, I learnt to embrace who I am with all my pros and cons. Transformational journeys are not to be measured in time or length; it is a lifelong process of self-knowledge and self-development.

A comfort zone is a beautiful place, but nothing ever grows there.

UNKNOWN AUTHOR

Personal growth really does come when we stretch ourselves to levels beyond our comfort zone, just as in exercise, where you need to create micro-tears in your muscles and feel pain to let your muscles grow and get stronger. People are generally not shy about sharing if they have muscle pain. We should not be shy to share our mental pain, doubts, worries and defeats if we want to become better leaders, and that is done with transparency, the third step in building your transformational journey to become a more reliable leader!

STEP 13: TRANSPARENCY

It is very difficult to be fully transparent as many leaders deal with so many issues – often confidential – so total transparency is of course not what we mean when we talk about this as a crucial step of your trustworthiness. In practice, bosses often keep information from certain team members and reveal it to others, independently of rank and status. It is a very human reaction as there is a natural character fit among people, and if one becomes the boss that natural tendency to trust some people more than others does not disappear. The absence of clear and transparent communication for everyone can create serious rumours and misinformation, which can undermine trust and morale. I have witnessed organizational cultures in which corridor information, guessing, and gossiping dominated.

I worked in an agency in which the information on becoming a partner was never communicated clearly, so we were all left to guess and interpret what we needed to do to reach that desirable status. Of course, it led to excessive flattery of the bosses by some of my colleagues who were also in the running to become a shareholder. Next to gaining the favour of the boss, back stabbing colleagues, bullying others, and a huge focus on internal politics was the most important task of the day for some of my colleagues. All because what it took to become a shareholder was unclear and never communicated to the contenders in a transparent way. I was very unhappy at this job and despite my high salary and promotion possibilities, I experienced firsthand how to become demotivated and disengaged.

Looking back at this experience, I wonder how much time and resources went into the wrong things. That agency faced a rapid decline and lost its market share and prestigious reputation. If we all had not been involved in the internal battle against each other, would its history have been different? No idea, but the cost of internal politics and untransparent moves of people in power is huge. Excessive internal politics in any organization can lead to a work environment where decisions are made based on personal agendas rather than in the best interests of the organization. This leads to suboptimal outcomes such as complicated decision-making processes, slower project execution, lost productivity and decreased operational efficiency and can lead to a disengaged workforce. Transparency is a cornerstone of trust. There is no denying this; it is a matter of finding how transparent you want to be and in which aspects of your business. Whatever your decision is on this point, make it an equal one for your team. By consistently sharing information, leaders show that they respect their team's capacity to handle the truth, even when it's challenging. This builds a strong bond of trust, crucial for effective leadership and teamwork. Being transparent about goals, strategies, and the reasoning behind decisions helps align the team towards common objectives. When team members understand the 'why' behind their tasks, they are more likely to engage deeply with their work and strive towards the shared vision. By embracing transparency, you can create a positive, trusting, and cooperative atmosphere that empowers individuals and teams to perform at their best. This approach not only enhances your reputation, but it also contributes to a more engaged and committed workforce.

Truth and transparency not only make you vulnerable but also build huge credibility.

JACK WELCH, FORMER CEO OF GENERAL ELECTRIC

Nonetheless, to be able to be transparent, you need to overcome one big hurdle, a hurdle many leaders are not able to take, and that is to accept showing vulnerability. There is a lot of strength in daring to show your vulnerable side, but let's face it, we have never been taught to do so. As soon as kids grow out of childhood, they are urged to stop crying, stop doubting, and start to act as adults. This is particularly true for boys. Society has taught men that talking about their emotions and being vulnerable is wrong. Expressions such as 'man up' can lead to suppressing emotions and even toxic masculinity. A leading voice in the conversation about masculinity and its evolving definition in modern society is author Richard Reeves.[95] Reeves's work is part of a growing dialogue that challenges outdated stereotypes and encourages a more nuanced understanding of what it means to be a man today. It would take me far too long to share his ideas about what is wrong with the boys and men in society, but his book *'Of Boys and Men'* is definitely an eye opener to understand why boys are falling behind in schools and why men are struggling in the labour market. Reeves advocates for a cultural shift that allows men to embrace vulnerability without fear of judgment or stigma, suggesting that such a change would benefit not only men themselves, but also broader society by fostering healthier, more supportive communities.

In short, transparency is a crucial part of building your reliable reputation towards your team and peers, and showing your vulnerable side can help you to gain trust. Transparency and vulnerability in leadership can lead to more authentic connections with team members, fostering a culture of trust, open communication, and mutual support. Leaders who embrace vulnerability often find that it enhances their effectiveness, encouraging a more collaborative and innovative team environment.

STEP 14: CULTURE AND VALUES

Ah, the importance of culture and values is finally here! There is so much to say about why it is crucial to have a good culture, but at the same time there is nothing so intangible as culture! Though every big organization has values, often they do not really live by them. Culture and values are deeply interrelated because they both shape and reflect the beliefs, behaviours, and norms within a society or group. What is the difference between culture and values? Culture and values are closely related concepts within organizations, but they are not the same thing.

Culture refers to the shared beliefs, attitudes, behaviours, and norms that characterise an organization. It's like the personality of the organization – the way things are done, the way people interact, and the overall vibe of the workplace. Culture often develops over time through shared experiences, interactions, and leadership styles within the organization. It can encompass aspects such as communication styles, decision-making processes, work environment, and employee morale. Culture is about behaviour and energy. Every organization has a culture; even a solo entrepreneur has a culture.

Values, on the other hand, are often defined only when organizations get bigger. They are the fundamental beliefs or Principles that guide the behaviour and decision-making of individuals within the organization. They represent what the organization stands for and what it considers important. Values serve as a moral compass for employees, helping them understand what behaviours are encouraged or discouraged within the organization. Values are about norms, beliefs, Principles, ethical choices and how you ideally want to care for others.

In summary, while culture encompasses the broader patterns of behaviour and interactions within an organization, values are the underlying Principles or ideals that shape and influence that culture. Values help define the desired behaviours and norms within the organizational culture.

Let's start with diving deeper into **culture**! One person can influence – both for the better or the worse – your organizational culture! It is something that can change overnight, in case for instance when layoffs are impacting the teams. But an organization can have several cultures; to promote engagement of teams, they are often allowed to craft their own culture, values, and purpose. This can be a differentiator to gain and retain talent! But culture can also implode a company! I witnessed this while I was working as a consultant for a prestigious and reputable investment corporation when that happened. I can assure you; it was not a pretty sight!

This investment company was big and successful, and the founder and CEO had created a culture of aggressive sales techniques and an overall winning mentality. When the first signs of troubles and mismanagement popped up in the press, the founder was forced to take a step back, and install a new CEO. The founder took a seat on the board of directors. This new CEO hired me to do a communication scan of their brand. In reality he wanted me to see how much damage had been done to the company because the rumours and press articles on a combination of aggressive business practices and possible fraud were harmful.

In a workshop with both the CEO, the founder and a number of team members, it was clear that this corporation was split into two camps. One camp was clearly a big fan of the founder and cheered at every move he made during the workshop, even if his moves, comments, and endless monologues were clearly designed to boycott the purpose of the workshop. The other camp wanted to support the new CEO and tried to take something from this session. It was a complete disaster! The founder completely hijacked the session by obstructing the meeting, to contest every exercise and to extend the afternoon lunch by ordering more wine than than was healthy for anyone. When half of the participants were late and too drunk to participate after lunch, I knew we had failed the assignment.

I had never witnessed a founder hijack his own company in such a destructive way. He was loud, obnoxious, disrespectful to many of us and acted like nobody could touch him. I was in deep shock and had no idea how to handle him. Nor did the new CEO, and nor did the team. The workshop ended and my report the next day with the CEO was honest and straightforward. I had no idea nor information at the time of the truth behind the allegations that the organization was poorly managed and engaged in risky financial activities. I did know, however, that the damage done to the brand, the toxic culture of aggressive business practices, that 'we are on top of the world' mentality of the sales team, and their superior attitude towards their colleagues at the firm was among the worst cultures I had ever seen.

I urged the new CEO to take a stand and install ethical standards on how to do business and treat both clients and employees. But with a founder who had installed this toxic culture and who was clearly still running the show, it was an impossible job for the newcomer. Not much later large-scale tax fraud, lack of adequate regulatory compliance, and personal legal issues of the founder led to the company's bankruptcy and serious legal consequences for the founder. He ended up in jail! Now I share this example as it was a textbook case of a CEO who had completely lost track of reality, who had surrounded himself with likeminded team leaders and who had created a culture of intimidation, of male toxicity, of bragging, drinking, showing off, and invincibility. I guess his favourite movie was *The Wolf of Wall Street*! I have nothing against a winning culture, but make it an inclusive one – one that is not based on bragging and male power play.

Creating a good and empowering organizational culture is a personal matter. But here are some key ingredients that you can define for yourself to craft a culture in which a diverse and multigenerational workforce can thrive:
- **Values matter:** We will talk more about it in the next step, but clearly define and communicate the core values that guide behaviour and decisions within the organization.
- **Lead by example:** Leadership should embody the culture they wish to foster, demonstrating commitment to organizational values through their actions.
- **Foster open communication:** Encourage a culture of transparency and open communication, where feedback is welcomed and valued at all levels.
- **Recognise and reward:** Consistently recognise and reward behaviour that aligns with the organizational values and goals, reinforcing the culture you wish to establish.

- **Promote teamwork:** Encourage collaboration and teamwork, ensuring that all employees feel they are part of a cohesive, supportive community.
- **Promote lifelong learning:** Commit to the continuous professional and personal development of employees, supporting their growth and aligning it with organizational goals.
- **Prioritise well-being:** Ensure that the well-being of employees is a priority, promoting a healthy work-life balance and providing support for mental and physical health.

These steps help in building a culture that not only attracts talent but also retains it by making the organization a great and caring place to work.

Let's now zoom in on the **value of values**!

The first thing I often notice about values is that companies have too many! Too often I meet up with CEOs who have trouble summing up all their values. They need to look at the wall on which they are written, or they need to retrieve them from their internet site. Once the HR director was called into the boss's office to cite them. This is not because these CEOs suffer from a loss of memory; they simply have overlooked a number of fundamental rules to consider when formulating values:

- **'Trop est trop'** as we say in French. Having too many values is difficult to remember. There are other elements in a strategic plan that leave room for additional aspects important to an organization. You can write a manifesto for instance, leaving you more room to talk about both your culture and values. You can write what you care for in your mission and vision statements. Your positioning statement also plays an important role in realising your business goals. So, for the sake of clarity, please keep your values to a minimum and make them short – ideally one word, and to the point. I always plead for three or four values maximum.
- **Relevant and authentic:** Words like 'quality' or 'operational excellence' are not values! Values are about beliefs and choices to care or strive for certain things. It is not about the bare minimum you expect from any company! Nobody ever says they don't want to offer quality, or they are lousy in customer service. So, forget about using generic words that are linked to business excellence and claiming them to be your values. Think more deeply

about what you really value as an organization, make it as relevant as possible for all and make sure it is authentic. Dare to choose quirky words if this fits your culture; it will make you stand out from the crowd even more.

- **Bottom-up/Top-down:** I am guilty of having crafted values with management teams during fancy strategic workshops. I was wrong at the time, and I have no issue in admitting this. Today I understand that values are something that need to be crafted, discussed, pondered and, if needed, adapted with all employees. It is an important driver of your talent strategy, and it is a crucial strategic pillar of your client strategy. Values matter, but they matter most when they are shared and lived by. Sure, this means it takes time to define the right values. The process can start at the top of an organization, but before finalising them, they absolutely need to be shared with your people to hear their feedback on them. This is a process that takes time and demands feedback. But if values are not shared, they are just generic, meaningless words.
- **Inclusiveness:** Seek input from diverse perspectives to ensure that the values represent the interests and values of all stakeholders. This can foster a sense of ownership and commitment to the values. It helps to bond internally over these values, and it helps to clearly communicate to the outside world what you stand for.
- **KISS: Keep it Simple, Stupid** is a rule that can really be applied to crafting values. Keep values clear, concise, and easy to understand. Avoid jargon or complex language that may confuse employees, clients, or stakeholders. Make sure that the values are memorable and easily communicated.
- **Actionable and measurable:** Make the values actionable by defining specific behaviours or actions that demonstrate each value in practice. This helps employees understand how to embody the values in their day-to-day work. Additionally, consider how the values can be measured or evaluated to assess their impact on organizational culture and performance.
- **Agility and adaptability:** As mentioned before, society and culture change fast, so recognise that values may evolve over time as the organization grows, faces new challenges, or responds to changes in the external environment. Be open to revisiting and refining the values periodically to ensure their continued relevance and effectiveness.

A second thing that strikes me when looking at organizational values: they are often so boring, serious, and generic! You don't want to know how many corporate value lists exist with values such as innovation, teamwork, integrity, accountability, and respect! Sure, all these words matter! But did you honestly not find a better and more distinctive way to say it?

Atlassian[96], an Australian software company uses a very direct and somewhat unconventional expression to emphasise the importance of customer respect and satisfaction. They have values like:
- Don't #@!% the customer.
- Open company, no bullshit.
- Play as a team.
- Build with heart and balance.
- Be the change you seek.

The Dutch Coolblue's core values are:
- Unconventional
- Friends
- Go for it
- Flexible

Values really matter; they define your conduct when things go well but, more importantly, when things go wrong. Especially in tough times, when people need to be fired, for instance, your values should guide you on how to do that. Many examples today still show us a different reality, unfortunately, but I have also witnessed cases in which the values bonded people together for life. In a podcast episode I discovered during Covid, Hilton's[97] CEO explained how they opened up their hotel rooms to 1 million frontline medical workers. Remember with lockdowns the tourism and leisure industry were down and hotels were empty, costing these organisations a fortune. Opening up the hotel chain and making even more costs for hosting the hospital staff was a decision the CEO took instantly. We need to focus on what matters, he said. Hilton's core values are hospitality, integrity, and leadership. We do the right thing, all the time, even at times when we bleed financially. That is a great example of how values can unite and make a powerful statement of care! That leads me to the final and important step of reliability and that is to be a supportive leader.

STEP 15: SUPPORT

Many leaders believe they are the highest in rank so they matter most. I gave many examples throughout the book of how consciously and unconsciously this happens. How it is facilitated by organizations, but also how it is demanded in certain cultures to actively demonstrate power and success. One of the many reasons why I love to work with Dutch people is that many of them do not express societal status through materialistic things. In 2021 the former prime minister Mark Rutte biked to the King's Palace to hand in his resignation letter. The foreign press could not believe their eyes and multiple videos of that moment can still be found online! When I worked at KPN, I was also very surprised to see my boss show up by bike at a team-building dinner in Amsterdam. Before starting to work in the Netherlands, I had never seen a boss on a bike! Status and mobility were shown through fancy cars! Today in many countries, many bosses arrive by bike luckily! Back to the point of feeling important: of course you can also claim your superior position in an organization on a bike!

Meanwhile, clever leaders know that they are only as good as the sum of their team. Contemporary and caring leaders know that by showing servant leadership, they get the best out of others, and also of themselves. It is way more comforting in this changing era to not carry the burden of business solely on your shoulders, but to share it with others. The best way to do that is to be of service to others, and that servant mentality starts inside by showing servant leadership to your teams. Of course this can go beyond your professional circle; you can be of service to your friends, family, community, city, or whatever societal role you want to take on. Servant leadership is a philosophy and set of practices that enriches the lives of individuals, builds better organizations, and ultimately create a more just and caring world. It's centred around the idea that the main goal of a leader should be to serve others.

Servant and supportive leadership is important for several reasons:

- **Empowerment:** Servant leaders prioritise the growth and development of their employees. By empowering their staff and providing them with the support, resources, and opportunities they need to succeed, servant leaders foster a culture of trust, collaboration, and innovation within the organization.
- **Engagement:** We discussed the importance of an engaged workforce at length, but when you serve your employees, you create a positive work environment where employees feel valued, respected, and motivated to contribute their best efforts. Servant leaders prioritise the growth and well-being of their people and the communities to which they belong. By focusing on the needs of team members, servant leaders help employees feel valued and respected. This leads to higher levels of employee engagement, job satisfaction, less burnout and bore-out, and a rise in loyalty to the organization.
- **Teamwork:** Servant leadership encourages a team-oriented approach to leadership, where leaders work alongside their team members to achieve shared goals. By fostering a sense of camaraderie, cooperation, and mutual respect, servant leaders build cohesive and high-performing teams that are capable of tackling complex challenges and driving organizational success. This type of leadership strengthens interpersonal relationships among team members, leading to better collaboration.
- **Ethical choices:** When understanding you are there to serve your team, your actions are grounded in values such as integrity, empathy, and ethical decision-making. Servant leaders prioritise the needs of others ahead of their own self-interest, demonstrating a commitment to ethical behaviour and social responsibility. This helps build trust with employees, stakeholders, and the broader community.
- **Resilience:** Something also mentioned before, but of utter importance in today's society in which so many people simply can't or refuse to adapt to the many and fast changes: create a supportive and nurturing work environment that helps employees thrive, even during challenging times. By providing emotional support, guidance, and encouragement, servant leaders help employees build resilience and adaptability, enabling them to overcome obstacles and bounce back from setbacks more effectively.

- **Enhanced trust, loyalty, and higher retention rates:** Servant leaders build trust by being transparent, listening to their employees, sharing power, and showing that they care about the team's interests as much as their own. This trust translates into deeper loyalty and commitment from team members. Companies with these leaders often experience lower turnover rates. When employees feel supported and know that their leaders are invested in their personal and professional growth, they are more likely to stay with an organization.
- **Success and overall higher performance:** While servant leadership focuses on the well-being of people, it also leads to better overall organizational performance. Engaged and satisfied employees are more productive, which can improve the quality of work and customer satisfaction.

Overall, servant leadership fosters a culture of service, empathy, and collaboration that drives employee engagement, teamwork, and organizational success in today's rapidly changing and complex business environment. By putting the needs of others first, servant leaders enhance individual and organizational capacities, leading to a more motivated, committed workforce and a more successful organization overall. A nice side effect is that it sets the tone for others as it has a positive societal impact. Give it a try. The exercises below will help you test it.

PODCAST INTERVIEW

WITH PROFESSOR ANDREAS RASCHE, PROFESSOR AND ASSOCIATE DEAN AT COPENHAGEN BUSINESS SCHOOL

Professor Andreas Rasche is a distinguished academic and thought leader. Renowned for his expertise in business ethics and corporate social responsibility, Professor Rasche has significantly contributed to the advancement of sustainable business practices. His scholarly work and practical insights bridge the gap between academic research and real-world application, influencing both academic circles and the business community.

Take Gen Z seriously; they want to be considered. That is what I can advise all business leaders.

ANDREAS RASCHE, PROFESSOR AND ASSOCIATE DEAN AT COPENHAGEN BUSINESS SCHOOL

As an Associate Dean, he plays a crucial role in shaping the strategic direction of the institution, fostering an environment that encourages innovative thinking and responsible management. Professor Rasche's commitment to ethical leadership and sustainability underscores his dedication to educating the next generation of business leaders who are equipped to tackle global challenges with integrity and foresight. The podcast interview with Andreas was a more generic talk about leadership in sustainability; still, his tips and insights are crucial.

Andreas Rasche's leadership tip:
- TIP 1: Know yourself before you start to show leadership to your team or society. Clarifying the relationship between yourself and sustainability is crucial. Where do you really stand on sustainability? What sacrifices are you willing to make?
- TIP 2: Have an honest conversation on this topic with yourself.

Spotify link to podcast episode

https://spotifyanchor-web.app.link/e/OwKLTrlwgMb

RELIABILITY EXERCISES

Safety: SHARE A SECRET

Team exercise

This is a great exercise before a workshop, a strategic offsite, an innovation session or anything that needs some out of the box thinking from the team. You start the meeting by asking the team members to write down something your team members don't know about you, on the same colour of post-it or the same card. The first reaction is often that you are an open book, and your colleagues know all about you. But when you think about it on a deeper level, there are always things your colleagues don't know about you. About your childhood, youth, parents, children, past hobbies, quirky habits, strange food preferences, illnesses, or other things you never thought about sharing at work. You put all the cards in a bowl or bag, and each team member draws a card randomly, and reads out loud what is written on it. Start the guessing game with the group whose colleague revealed this.

Purpose of this exercise: to discover on a deeper level something about your colleagues. This knowledge, often combined with fun while discovering the secrets, connects colleagues on a deeper level, as these 'secrets' often involve emotions we rarely share at work. This deeper connection on an emotional level will create an extra level of psychological safety.

Authenticity: THE ANSWERING GAME

Solo exercise

Set the intention for yourself to say to a colleague (or your boss) 3 times in a week: 'I don't know'. Dare to be honest when you really don't know and give compliments when colleagues also admit that they don't know.

Purpose of this exercise: to be open and transparent about your knowledge, solution-driven answers, and ability to always come up with an answer, even though in reality you doubt that it is the right answer. Discover also what this 'I don't know' answer does to your team members.

Do they step in and find a solution themselves? Do they ask for advice from others? What is the impact of your authentic 'I don't know' answer to the group dynamics?

Transparency: DOES IT WORK?

Duo exercise
Can be done after every project or collaboration as mutual evaluation/feedback. Sit together and bring a piece of paper (post-it) and a pen. Be quiet and reflect for a few minutes on the project you collaborated on. This exercise is not to judge a project, but to think about the collaboration.

Write the following two sentences and answer them.

'What works for me in our collaboration?'

'What doesn't work for me in our collaboration?'

Please note: Be concrete and specific. Avoid judgment and the desire to change the other. Take personal responsibility for your experience in the collaboration. This is not criticism of or toward your colleague.

After you have both written your feedback, read aloud without any further explanation, no defence and without starting a conversation. Hand the feedback over and the receiver only replies: 'Thank you'.

Purpose of this exercise: to learn to specifically give feedback and understand that this is your experience, rather than the need to change the other person. Learn to be open and transparent, no matter the role or position of the person you are dealing with. This mutual feedback session is not meant to criticise the other but to grow together and create a reliable work environment in which everybody feels psychologically safe to share experiences.

Culture: START-STOP-CONTINUE TASK

Solo exercise for the team leader

Culture is a top-down intangible thing, so you as a team leader have a big influence on it. Think about your organizational culture. Take a paper and write down: what goes well, what is essential to it, and what could be better? Write down this list of things that you have noticed.

Divide that list into at least three things you want to start. New things you want to try out to make the culture better. Things you want to change in your leadership style to influence your team for the better. The next list is a minimum of three things you want to stop. Bad habits that settled in. Behaviour you don't like, but that always come out under stress. Make it very concrete, even if it is small habits you want to stop. They will influence your team. The final list is made up of three things minimum you want to continue. Things that work well, both for you and your team. Things that are fundamental for the smooth functioning and well-being of yourself and your team. The next step is to remind yourself during a month – each day – of these lists. Are you making progress? What is easier said than done? How do you feel about these changes? Does it make you a better leader? Is the culture evolving for the better? In a good culture, share this exercise with your team after a month, and dare to ask them if they felt the change. Ask them for feedback and suggestions on how they can contribute to make the organizational culture even better.

Purpose of this exercise: to help leaders recognise discrepancies between their declared values and their actual behaviours, promoting a stronger alignment between what they say (talk) and what they do (walk).

Support: THE BUDDY BACK-UP

Duo exercise

Share an aspect of yourself that you would like to get better at, a learning opportunity you see for yourself. Who of your colleagues or bosses is very good at what you would like to get better at?

What are you good at, which your colleague or boss could learn from you? Who would you like to buddy up with to teach you that skill or trait?

Select that person and ask him/her for a buddy challenge.

Challenge each other and catch up on a regular basis to learn from the progress you both make, but also to receive support of your learning curve along the way. Understand better the pitfalls you are facing, and receive constructive feedback from each other.

Make sure you give each other a challenge as a commitment to learn.

Purpose of this exercise: in support mode, you dare new things, and you become more accountable as you do it. Your buddy is there to guide you and support you. The challenge makes it fun and concrete.

Can't wait to read about
EMPATHY?

20	EQUALITY
19	APPRECIATION
18	ACTIVE LISTENING
17	ENGAGEMENT
16	INTROSPECTION

EMPATHY

PLAY SECTION 8
EMPATHY MATTERS

The term 'empathy' is fairly recent: it has only been around for about a century. Today it is actively studied by many cognitive and social psychologists, and we still have a lot to learn. It was probably Brene Brown[98] who made talking about vulnerability and empathy conventional. A research professor at the University of Houston, she has spent decades studying courage, vulnerability, shame, and empathy. Her 2011 TED Talk[99] made her instantly popular! This video has been viewed over 21 million times. When I wrote my first book, the views amounted to 14 million. The rising importance and attention to empathy is great as I still see a lot of eyebrows raised when I talk about empathy.

According to Anita Nowak, a Canadian specialist in empathy, with a PhD in the field, empathy is our superpower. She defines empathy as a profound human capacity that can be cultivated for personal, organizational, and social transformation. She views empathy not just as an emotional response but as a skill that can be intentionally developed and used to drive change. Nowak emphasises the importance of 'purposeful empathy', which involves using empathy deliberately to create positive impacts and promote understanding and compassion among people. Her approach highlights empathy as a powerful tool for leadership and change, advocating for its active development in individuals and organizations to enhance relationships, foster inclusiveness, and address societal challenges effectively. This perspective positions empathy as both a personal trait and a strategic element in achieving broader goals, underscoring its potential as a transformative force in various contexts.

Professor in psychology Dr. Theresa Wiseman's four defining attributes of empathy are:[100]

- to be able to see the world as others see it
- to be non-judgmental
- to understand another person's feelings and
- to communicate your understanding of that person's feelings.

Since the CARE Principles were created as a human-centric strategic framework, it is only logical that encouraging people to think about how they can become more empathic is one of its strategic Principles. You may not think that empathy will make a difference to your business today, but it will undeniably give you a head start in tomorrow's world.

Empathy is considered a soft skill by many people. Sure, I get it. Empathy is considered a soft skill because it pertains to the way people handle interpersonal relations and communicate effectively with others. Soft skills are typically contrasted with hard skills, teachable abilities that can be defined and measured, such as typing, writing, math, reading, and the ability to use software programs. Soft skills are less tangible and harder to quantify, encompassing personal attributes, communication abilities, and emotional intelligence. But don't be misled by the term 'soft' skill; empathy is hard work, as it requires being vulnerable. And vulnerability is a skill that we have been encouraged to unlearn in business. Being a great business leader has always been about 'power', 'control', 'project success', and more male external traits of making it in the hard world of business.

Empathy involves understanding and sharing the feelings of others, which plays a crucial role in building relationships, facilitating communication, and fostering a collaborative work environment. It enables individuals to navigate social complexities, lead teams more effectively, and create positive interactions. Although often harder to measure directly than hard skills, empathy significantly impacts organizational success and personal effectiveness in social settings. As such, it's highly valued in various professional and personal contexts, and it is about time to start to work that empathy muscle to get better at it! In an age when technology drives many processes and AI powered computers become our colleagues, the human side of work will matter more than ever. Our relationships with colleagues, clients, suppliers, and business partners will play a major role in the success of our organizations.

To my disbelief, I saw an organization slide from very empathetic to non-empathetic in just a few months. What happened? The CEO – a very empathetic people leader – had left the company. Before he left the organization, the culture felt warm, and people loved to work for this brand. That was my genuine feeling when I started to work for them. The CARE Scan conducted for the European branches affirmed the great internal culture and the firm being a great place to work. The management and employees were on the same page and gave similar scores, indicating a shared corporate culture. By comparison, in the Belgian benchmark, management consistently gives their company higher scores than employees in most areas. The CARE Scan revealed very high scores on CARE for their own people, considerably higher than the benchmark. Their internal empathy scores were very high and admirable, rarely seen in the CARE Scan! Unfortunately, as soon as the CEO had left the building, the organization was left in doubt as to who the new CEO would be. This was an American company, and the appointment of the new CEO took longer than foreseen, leaving the European organization floating like a boat with no captain. A combination of cost-cutting orders, operating in difficult market circumstances after Covid, and no new boss turned this organization completely upside down in terms of culture and empathy. It was frightening to see how culture and values can leave the building together with the CEO. It has taught me that the opposite can also happen; a new boss can change an average culture around too. A boss really has that power if they want!

I kid you not

With more diverse and multigenerational teams, empathy is for sure a key skill to learn, and your brain and body will reward you for it! When we show empathy, several key hormones and neurotransmitters are released in the brain that facilitate emotional bonding and social connection. Here are some of the primary ones:
- **Oxytocin:** Often referred to as the 'love hormone', oxytocin is released during moments of closeness and bonding. It plays a significant role in social behaviour and is known to increase trust and reduce fear, making it easier to connect with others and show empathy.

- **Dopamine:** This neurotransmitter is associated with the pleasure centre of the brain. When we engage in empathetic behaviour and feel the satisfaction of helping others or connecting with them on an emotional level, dopamine is released, which reinforces these behaviours by providing a sense of pleasure and reward.
- **Endorphins:** These are the body's natural painkillers and contribute to feelings of well-being. They can be released when we engage in empathetic interactions, helping to elevate our mood and reduce stress.
- **Serotonin:** This neurotransmitter helps regulate mood and social behaviour. Low levels of serotonin are associated with depression and difficulty in forming social bonds, whereas increased serotonin levels can improve mood and promote feelings of well-being, which are important for empathetic engagement.

A combination of these hormones and neurotransmitters creates a biochemical environment in the brain that supports empathy, encouraging bonding, and improving overall social interactions. Showing care and empathy for others is honestly one of the most fulfilling things to do. All research[101] proves that people feel happier and more balanced when they feel connected to others. When your brain gives you little shots of happiness, your body will feel great too, because we know that mental and physical well-being is interconnected. With a more diverse and multigenerational workforce, with more burnout and people who simply can no longer cope with the stress, pressure, and anxiety the world is giving us, you would think it would be easy for us all to start to show more empathy, right? Unfortunately, there are still many hurdles ahead of us.

EMPATHY HURDLES

Although empathy seems like a basic human ability, consistent research over the past few years shows that empathy is in decline among people of all ages around the world.[102] One reason for this could be our own brain and it could be seen as the opposite of what you read just above. When you think about yourself, talk about your own priorities, or are confirmed by others, your brain releases dopamine. Remember dopamine is a neurotransmitter often associated with pleasure, motivation, and reward. That might explain why so many leaders like to surround themselves with like-minded people who confirm their opinions. When this happens, or when you are reflecting on yourself, busy with your ego, or simply explaining your own thoughts and others confirm that, your brain's reward system is activated, and releases dopamine.

This explains why many leaders prefer monologues to dialogues! The release of dopamine in their brain when this happens can make them feel good, motivated and satisfied. This can get addictive, as the Dutch author Lammert Kamphuis[103] said. In his opinion, we need to be aware of this trick of our brain, and he offers more insights and exercises on how to deal with this addiction to the ego! As conflicting as it may sound with the happy chemicals your body also releases when we show empathy for others, it is good to understand that our behaviour is not always as straightforward as we would like it to be.

A second reason for a decline in empathy could be related to technology: we all spend a fair amount of time with our noses buried in our smartphones and glued to our screens. This encourages us to live inside our digital bubble, without much emotional awareness of others. Social media is purposefully designed to make us addictive. Next to infinite scroll mechanisms that endlessly feed us new content, the platforms employ a psychological concept known as variable reward, where users receive unpredictable positive feedback. Each swipe or refresh can bring up something new and exciting, much like pulling a lever on a slot machine. This unpredictability is compelling and can lead to users spending more time on the app. Other tricks like social feedback loops, push notifications and ease of self-content creation are designed to keep users busy on the platform. Social media can for sure have pleasurable effects, however their addictive methods have a negative impact on many people's mental health and productivity.

Although there is no academic agreement yet on the negative impact of social media on the mental health of youngsters, the signs are there that since the launch of Instagram in 2010, US youngsters[104] have less real-life contact with their friends, which affects their state of mind. The more time they spend on social media, the worse their mental health gets. The effect on girls is the worst and can lead to negative psychological impacts including self-harm. Rates of suicide have climbed steeply since 2010 on both sides of the Atlantic.

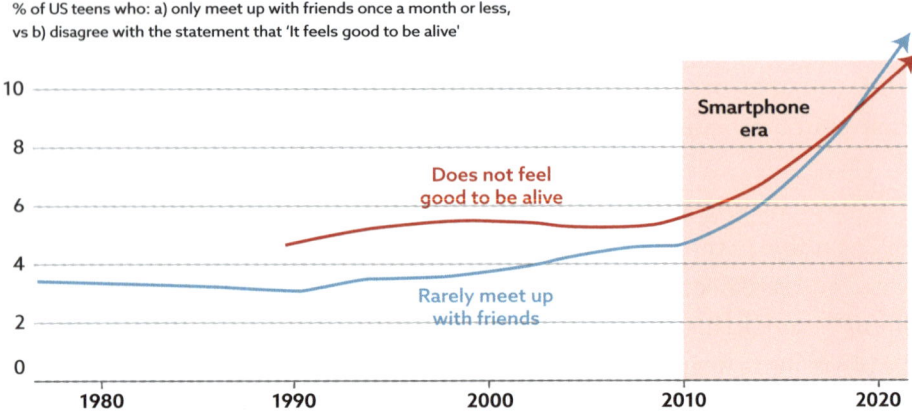

Figure 11: Two measures of mental health among US teens over time. The share of US teens who only meet up with friends once a month or less has rocketed in the last decade, tracking worsening mental health

The more time we spend in the online world, the less we see and meet people in the real world. Combine this with the reality tunnel explained before and as result, people are driven further and further apart. Social isolation, loneliness and a decline in empathy all go hand in hand.

The world seems to be splitting into opposite camps and media fuels these oppositions and polarises people who preach it: left versus right, conservative versus liberal, black versus white, poor versus rich, woke versus anti-woke, pro versus contra. Nuance seems to have left the building, leaving little or no empathy or understanding for others' point of view. Nuance is also not easily explained in a seven-second eye-catching video on TikTok or statement on X. People's brains are made numb by snackable content and over-simplifying concepts. While we all know that reality is never black or white. The content fed to us on social media can be compared to junk food. It creates spikes of dopamine, it affects our attention span, making sustained focus on a single task like listening to others more challenging over time.

Yet according to other research on empathy at work, more than 90% of employees, HR professionals and CEOs state that empathy is important. In business, however, empathy is still rarely spotted. An empathic boss might be considered weak by some. Despite a great deal of research proving that empathy matters, many managers try to keep empathy away from the work floor. It is often overlooked as a leadership value, perhaps because it's seen as too soft or too nice. People equate empathy with niceness, although it is not the same thing at all! One reason for this may be linked to the alpha-male business culture that still prevails throughout several industries. Big corporations like France Telecom, Uber, VRT and even Nike[105] have been accused of misconduct, bullying and sexual harassment. This type of toxic, non-inclusive leadership leaves no room for a value like empathy. It creates a 'winner takes all' mentality that produces organizational dysfunction, with employees treating each other ruthlessly in the scramble to get ahead.

Today, 72% of American CEOs agree that empathy can drive business results; however, that same study[106] shows an 'empathy gap', meaning a *lot of leaders are talking the talk, but are failing to walk the walk!* As empathy in the workplace is relatively new, many CEOs say they struggle to consistently exhibit empathy in the workplace, and their employees agree. Many business leaders believe their own company is empathetic, but their staff often disagrees. This disconnect shows that empathy is something that needs to be learnt and acted upon, day in, day out. Since the discovery and implementation of empathy in business is still relatively new, the empathy economy is booming. Coaches offering empathy workshops – for a hefty price – are coming out of the woodwork. Be aware, too, that some companies may also try to 'empathy-wash' their message in the same way others 'greenwash' their marketing to look more environmentally friendly.

> ### Empathy is the innate trait that unites us in our shared humanity.
> **ANITA NOWAK, AUTHOR AND PHD EXPERT IN EMPATHY**

Empathy can be misused for narrow or short-sighted goals, and, at worst, can even be seen as manipulation. The greatest risk of empathy-washing is that empathy is at a risk of being devalued, as it might be abused by too many leaders trying to sugar-coat reality. Probably the biggest empathy hurdle is stress. It is scientifically proven that several neurobiological processes like cortisol release occur in the brain and affect our capacity for empathy. Stress also leads to increased activity in the amygdala, the part of the brain involved in emotional processing and threat detection. When the amygdala is hyper-activated, it can dominate other brain processes, leading to more reactive and less reflective responses. This state can make it difficult to engage in empathetic processing, as the brain is more focused on addressing perceived threats.

These and more changes in the brain illustrate why during periods of high stress, people might seem more self-centred, less compassionate, or less understanding of others' feelings. It's a natural response intended to prioritise one's own immediate survival and problem-solving over social engagement and emotional connection. However, recognising these effects can help in developing strategies to maintain empathy and social connection even during stressful times.

Before I dive further into the five essential steps of empathy, you might want to listen to Anita Nowak. I had the honour of interviewing her about the crucial role of empathy, and she explains in such a great way how our brain works. Not only when we are stressed, but also how the brain rewards us to show empathy. Check out this podcast interview below this play section.

No time for a podcast break? Save it for later! May I ask your empathy by granting me a small act of kindness? Please follow, subscribe, or simply share my podcast to other innovators and contemporary leaders. My podcast is taking me a lot of time, and I love that because I learn so much myself from the leaders I interview, but as I finance my podcast myself, the time I spend on it is like a pro-bono investment! Simply by subscribing to my podcast, I can extend my range and grow my reach and that is what my ultimate goal is: to reach more business leaders and show them how the CARE Principles can help them become the best IN and FOR the world. Thank you!

WHAT DOES THE BENCHMARK STUDY ON THE CARE PRINCIPLES REVEAL?

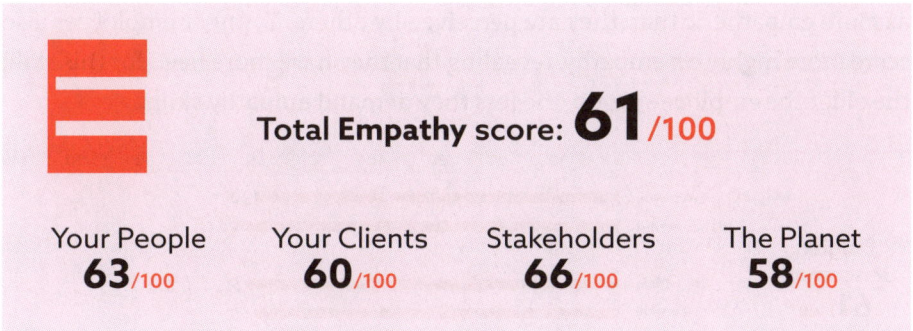

Figure 12: Care Scan empathy scores.

With a total score on empathy of 61% you could say that Belgian companies are not the worst at showing they truly care for others and know how to express that care. But when you look more closely at these numbers, it is strange to see that stakeholders score higher in empathy scores – 66% – compared to clients: 60% and your employees: 63%. Throughout the whole benchmark study on all pillars of CARE, 'Care for the Planet' has the lowest scores. Hopefully the Green Deal laws and regulations in combination with more people who demand a more sustainable approach from businesses will move the needle upwards on this topic!

A close look at some questions about empathy for their own people reveals that 66% of Belgian employees somewhat or completely agree that their company cares about a good work-life balance, compared to 23% who somewhat or strongly disagree. 59% of Belgian employees agree that the management genuinely sympathises with them; 28% disagree with this statement. 70% state that they feel safe expressing and being themselves, compared to 20% of the working population who don't agree with that. These statistics are encouraging and show that, in most companies, management is doing a great job.

Where we see room for improvement is in the fields where empathy is shown for instance in equal positive and negative feedback. 31% of employees receive both praise and tips on how to do better. 34% of them say that the feedback is mainly on mistakes. Another interesting insight from the benchmark study is that it reveals how management gives themselves a higher score on empathy compared to employees. Probably because people generally tend to think of themselves as more empathetic than they are perceived by others. Younger employees also score more highly on empathy, revealing that they have more need for this skill; the older the employee group, the less they demand empathy skills.

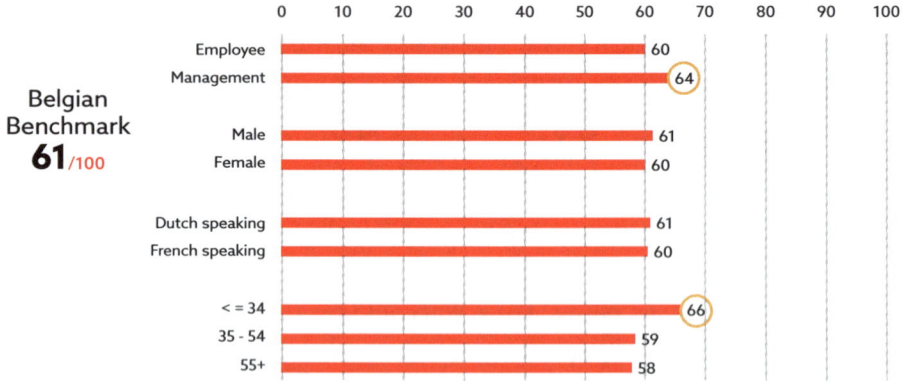

The Empathy Score is higher among management and younger employees.

Figure 13: Care Scan comparative scores for empathy.

I am curious about how the benchmark study will continue to evolve, something Ivox will monitor over time. Curious how your organization scores? Simply contact Ivox and they can set up your CARE Scan in just a few easy steps for organizations all over Europe. With no further ado, here are the five essential steps for empathy.

THE 5 ESSENTIAL STEPS OF EMPATHY

STEP 16: DARE TO OPEN UP TO INTROSPECTION

Introspection might be the hardest part of empathy when I think about it. We all know that habit – I certainly do – of immediately starting to blame others when something goes wrong in our lives.

I am late to a meeting, not because I should have gotten up earlier and checked my Waze. Nope, I blame traffic and lousy drivers who cause accidents. When I can't convince a prospect to start to work with me, I convince myself they do not understand the CARE Principles. It takes courage to admit my sales techniques might suck. When something goes wrong, anywhere frankly, the first thing we do is try to find who to blame. Pointing fingers at others is our favourite sport. I know bosses who only show up on the work floor to come and point to those who made mistakes. On all other occasions when these people do their jobs correctly, nobody shows up to praise them. Does that sound familiar?

Many people – again I can include myself in this category – even prefer lying to introspection. We often prefer to tell white lies – those small, seemingly harmless untruths – instead of seeking for and telling the truth. It is often an unconscious internal process that leads to these small white lies. Nothing harmful, habits that grew on us, or simply social conditioning are reasons why we don't consider the deeper implications or explore alternative, more honest responses to ourselves. Introspection can sometimes lead to uncomfortable truths about oneself or one's situation. Avoiding introspection may lead to using white lies as an easy escape from facing these truths or dealing with the emotional discomfort they might bring.

It can result in a diminished sense of personal accountability. If we do not regularly examine our actions and our impact on others, we might be less concerned about the potential negative consequences of telling white lies. Frankly, without introspection, there might be an over-reliance on social norms or the desire for social approval, ignoring our personal ethical choices, and moral compass. Finally, introspection helps people understand how their behaviour affects others; without it, this could ultimately undermine trust and authenticity in their relationships. Why is blaming others versus introspection so deeply rooted in humanity? Why is it so difficult? Why do we see so little of it in leadership and management roles?

Many people:

- **Like self-preservation:** From an evolutionary standpoint, protecting one's self-image and self-esteem is crucial. Blaming others can be a defence mechanism that protects an individual's self-concept by externalising failures and negative outcomes. This prevents the internal discomfort that might come from acknowledging one's own faults or shortcomings.
- **Have trouble showing vulnerability:** This is still considered as a weakness – certainly in a professional context. Leaders are afraid that it might open them to the risk of exploitation by people inside and outside of the organization. The current bosses have been raised under older role models who certainly showed a legacy of 'strong' leadership as a sign of professionalism. Vulnerability mistakenly might be seen as the incapacity to make decisions.
- **Are socially and culturally conditioned:** In many cultures, there is a strong emphasis on success and achievement, and failure is stigmatised. This can lead to a culture of blame, where it's safer socially and psychologically than to accept personal responsibility, which might be seen as admitting weakness or inadequacy.
- **Lack emotional intelligence:** Emotional intelligence includes self-awareness and self-regulation. It has historically been stereotyped as a more 'feminine' trait. A choice for leaders with a high IQ rather than a well-developed EQ or a balanced IQ-EQ ratio is still a reality at many C-level positions.
- **Lack courage:** It's often painful to confront one's own mistakes, shortcomings, or the role one played in a negative outcome. Blaming others can be a shortcut that avoids these difficult emotions and the responsibility of making amends or changes. It takes real courage to see your true self, not your projected self.
- **Learned how to play the power game:** Blaming others can also be a way to exert control or assert dominance in relationships or situations. By placing blame, an individual positions themselves as a victim or a judge, potentially manipulating the narrative to their advantage. If you grow up in environments where blame is a common response to problems, you may learn to model this behaviour unconsciously. Blaming becomes a habitual response to any conflict or failure.

Introspection is hard but necessary as it helps you become a more authentic person. You learn more from mistakes than from faking or blaming. I worked for years in a company where 'fake it till we make it' was the claim from the management. I know how successful this is. Still, I never believed in and participated in this culture as deep down it felt wrong. But the courage and self-knowledge it takes to be yourself, remain yourself and first think about what you have done, before naturally starting to blame others, is a lifelong process. One I frankly still have a lot to learn about, even if I understand how important a Principle it is to be truly empathetic towards others.

STEP 17: ENGAGEMENT

Gallup's research in 2023 reveals that, globally, over 50% of the workforce is considered disengaged, contributing to an $8.8 trillion economic cost. You would think that by now employers would understand the difficult but important art of saying goodbye to their staff. Exit conversations, procedures for resignations, and following the rules and regulations seems like the obvious choice when you need to let people go for whatever reason, right? Think again, as power brands like Tesla have a terrible and longstanding reputation for laying off people without warning them. Despite lawsuits[107] against them, in their 2024 layoff round of showing 10% of their global staff the door, they persisted in the horrendous uncaring practice of not informing people that they had been fired. Cutting jobs and getting laid off by email is a poor people management style, but instances of employees showing up at work and finding out that they had been fired because their badge didn't work continue to happen at Tesla.

But not only Tesla is guilty; most big tech companies[108] like Google, Meta, Twitter, and Microsoft have textbook examples of how NOT to deal with employees when you lay them off. The lack of empathy could not be worse than when Microsoft hosted a private concert by Sting at Davos, the night before firing 10,000 people. Finding out via email or auto-shut-out that you have lost your job is brutal for anyone. Employees no longer accept this and tell the world about it through loud quitting.

You could argue that job cuts are sometimes necessary for the overall health of the company. I fully agree, but the way you let go of people needs to be done with respect and empathy – and not only for the damage poor layoff practices can do to your brand's reputation. It is also of utter importance for your remaining staff. Firstly, because your employees develop friendships and camaraderie and when you lose your friends at work, this creates tension among those who remain too. But there is more to it. When people understand that the organization is cutting jobs, and communication is poor and non-transparent about how many people need to leave or why, the remaining employees get scared that their head is next to be chopped off. This not only kills morale, but it has a tremendously negative impact on your employee engagement, culture, and values.

The most value-driven organizations have a great culture, and during layoffs employees watch carefully what remains of that. People are no longer fooled by shiny employee manifestos when none of those words matters during tough times when people are fired. When you need to fire people, I challenge you to think about the effect it will have both on the people that you fire, and on those who remain in their seat. However, in today's typical organization, most employees are neither engaged nor actively disengaged. They are filling a seat but have yet to take ownership of their work. By not engaging these employees, leaders are missing a primary driver of customer retention and organic business growth as an indifferent employee is something that is also felt by clients. You must have felt the same when you contact customer care, and that employee is genuinely nice and helpful. This happens so rarely that it immediately gives you a better feeling about that organization, and I am sure that next time you will spend your money with them.

Let's set the record straight on a misconception. Employee engagement[109] does not mean happiness. If you are only measuring employee contentment, you are missing engagement. And the reality is that many corporate measures of engagement are just measuring contentment.

True engagement means:
- your people are psychologically present to do their work.
- They understand what to do.

- They have what they need to fulfil their job.
- They have a supportive manager.
- They feel part of a supportive team.
- They know why their work matters.
- They know why they get out of bed every morning and that is for more than just earning money.
- You share a purpose and that drives engagement!

According to Gallup's research, the global average is about one engaged employee for every one actively disengaged employee. To nobody's surprise the manager is the cornerstone of engagement. 70% of team engagement is attributable to the manager.

Unfortunately, the study continues with the fact that many of your managers are quiet quitting too:
- They are waiting for the tools to build great teams.
- Their concerns are not listened to.
- They are not feeling appreciated themselves.
- The highest level does not feel supported by the board of directors.
- The board of directors seldom has ears for the complexity of managing teams today.
- Most of the focus and discussions are about numbers, market share, costs, and margins.

One of the taboos that still exists is that many CEOs feel lonely, and this loneliness can lead to disengagement in the highest position of the organization. CEOs are still considered to have superpowers, know it all, always be on top of their game, show no doubt or weakness and only make the right decisions. In return for their high pay cheque, we expect quite supernatural powers from them. But they remain humans after all. It is still rare to witness a board of directors that pays attention to the mental well-being of the CEO, or that grants them a healthy work-life balance. They need to be strong and outspoken about what they need to remain healthy and in balance to perform. Only rarely does someone above or below them truly care about them.

Luckily it became more common practice to reach out to others like coaches and mentors as lifelines to battle the loneliness[110] and emotional burden of guiding a company. Research from the Graduate School of Business highlighted that nearly half of CEOs experience feelings of loneliness that they believe hinders their performance. These perspectives underscore the need for support systems and resources for individuals in high-pressure leadership roles, recognising that the stress and isolation they experience can have real implications for both their personal well-being and their company's performance. One could say that there is an engagement crisis throughout all levels within an organization. Low morale, decreased productivity, high turnover rates, and a general disconnection from the organization's goals and values is a reality for more people than you would expect. If an organization is indeed facing an engagement crisis, it needs to address underlying issues such as leadership style, recognition, workload balance, alignment with company values, and opportunities for growth and development.

Engagement in empathy is fundamental in building and sustaining meaningful and healthy relationships, fostering collaboration and teamwork, and creating compassionate teams. When leaders appreciate their employees, it can lead to higher levels of job satisfaction and engagement. Engaged employees are more likely to invest discretionary effort in their work, go beyond job requirements, and contribute to organizational success. Engaging your people can be done by something that seems simple, but proves to be very difficult, and that is listening – actively and wholeheartedly.

STEP 18: ACTIVE LISTENING

Most of us say we are good listeners, or at least that is what we think about ourselves. We have ears, we have that basic ability to understand what the other is saying, right? Let's start with getting one incorrect preconception out of the way. Listening is not the same as hearing. According to Thomas Neal who has a popular Ted Talk[111] on this subject, hearing is a function. Listening is a desire. I love that explanation. It is a skill, something we can train for, and something that we actively need to keep on doing, as it is not like cycling, which you can do for the rest of your life once you have learned how.

Simon Sinek admitted that he was in shock when his girlfriend told him he was a bad listener. He has built a global reputation as a business coach, his books are filled with advice on the importance of active listening as a skill of leadership – and his girlfriend accused him of being a bad listener himself. He mentioned in a podcast that he denied it at first, but through introspection understood that although he makes a living out of active listening, he indeed was bad at it in his personal life. It is a skill he developed for his career, not his love life. A shocking conclusion, right? But so humble of Sinek to share that with his audience.

Why is active listening necessary if you want your organization to thrive and grow? Active listening is about truly listening to what others are saying, not just to the words but also to understand the emotions and intentions behind them. This helps in accurately perceiving another's emotional state. This is hard because we are proven to be bad listeners overall. While we listen, we are often already searching for answers in our heads. We are waiting for an opening in between the words of the other to jump in and say whatever we find necessary. Often our answer is completely off and besides the point. It is an answer that we formulated without really considering what the other mentioned. If you start to actively pay attention to this, both in your own conversations and while watching others interact, it is staggering to see how many answers we give, without having heard the other. I'm ashamed to admit that I also have trouble focusing my brain on listening, and not on already engaging in finding answers.

And that is just the start of the challenge to active listening. Imagine all the external things that have an impact on your listening skills; you are in a noisy room, you feel cold, the other person is repeating the same thing over and over again, to your frustration, you need to pee, you are hungry, you get stressed as your to-do list is not getting any shorter simply sitting here and listening, you did not plan for this conversation to happen, you want to exercise more, you want to stop drinking, your kid's dental appointment is still not fixed... Recognise this? Various sources suggest that humans experience thousands of thoughts per day, with some estimates ranging from 50,000 to 70,000 thoughts daily, all of them interfering with your listening skills.

So it is fair to say that active listening is hard, because it requires multiple cognitive processes that go beyond just hearing words. It involves truly understanding, processing, and responding thoughtfully to what's being said. It also demands patience and an openness to understanding that we all have biases and preconceived notions that can filter or distort what we hear. Active listening requires setting these aside to understand the speaker's message as they intend it. To become better at active listening, it helps to practise mindfulness, manage distractions, and consciously engage in the listening process. Being aware of the challenges is the first step in improving this critical communication skill. What else can help you to hone this important skill? Train yourself in:

- **Paying attention to nonverbal communication:** Body language, eye contact, facial expressions, and other nonverbal cues provide insights into how someone is feeling.
- **Being non-judgmental:** Approach others' feelings and experiences with an open mind, without quick judgments or evaluations that can hinder true empathetic engagement.
- **Responding appropriately:** After understanding and connecting with another's emotions, responding in a way that is supportive and appropriate to the situation can validate their experiences and contribute to resolution or comfort.
- **Simply getting into the mud with the other:** A nice phrase used by Simon Sinek to express what he asks from his colleagues and friends when he is struggling with something: he just wants them to listen, not even reply. Very often people know what they need to do to get out of whatever situation they are in; they just need to ventilate their pain, frustration, grief, feelings of failure, or stress. So, in many cases, simply sitting with them in the mud and being present is the best way to showcase active listening!
- **Not allowing your phone or devices to distract you:** You can't focus on people's stories and their verbal and non-verbal signals when you are constantly being beeped at by push notifications or incoming mails or messages. Ideally, go for a walk without phones while listening to your team member to fully embrace the worries they share.

Finally, a word about the need of younger and diverse generations to be heard. 'Don't we listen already, all the time? I feel I listen too much, and have no time left to work,' a boss who works with Millennials and Gen Z told me recently. 'Younger generations need so much attention and the need to share all of their worries is so time consuming,' she continued. 'They all have psychologists, and they are open about this, to my surprise,' she added. 'Must I really play their psychologist at work too? I just want them to focus on work.' I must admit that younger generations share more things at work than we ever did! I must admit that it is hard for the C-level to deal with all the socio-economical, ecological, cultural challenges and on top of that the requirement to listen to a generation that is so vocal about their thoughts and behaviour.

When you look at the mental health of people, you understand the necessity to listen to people. A Eurobarometer survey[112] conducted in June 2023 revealed that almost one in two people (46% of the EU population) had experienced emotional or psychosocial problems, such as feeling depressed or anxious, in the previous 12 months. When you add loneliness statistics to this – 20% of school-going kids between 16 and 25 years old suffer from loneliness in Europe[113] – you understand the need of these generations to ventilate their worries.

If you work with these generations, active listening is definitely a skill to develop as they are looking for environments that stimulate open dialogues about all subjects. They often prioritise personal and career development, expecting leaders to actively listen and respond to their needs and aspirations to help them grow within the organization.

Finally, they are looking for appreciation and recognition, and that leads me to the fourth step into a more empathetic leadership style. It might also help them if you warn them about the unhealthy and addictive mechanisms behind social media. Of course they will not want to give up their devices, but educating them to spend less time online, and more time offline is a great first step in helping them build resilience.

STEP 19: APPRECIATION

Again, appreciation might seem something so simple and easy to give, but in reality we find it easier to pinpoint what has gone wrong than to praise what has gone well. It actually starts with education. How many parents still raise kids with the threat of punishment? If you don't do X, you won't get Y. You know what I mean, right! Strange, because from a strictly psychological and educational standpoint,[114] it has been proven that praise is far more effective and has a more positive impact than punishment on children. Giving physical and audible rewards of praise boosts self-esteem, helps the child's emotional growth and is more likely to produce the desired behaviour you want in your children. The educational system however also is based on what you don't know, rather than what you know. Red pens cross out wrong answers and multiple-choice exams try to trick you into giving the wrong answers. Some professors are proud of their reputations of only letting a tiny percentage succeed in the first sitting.

This widespread mentality extends into the work environment as we have officialised the one evaluation meeting per year. Most evaluation meetings – independently of the size of the company or the sector – come down to the same game: the employee only wants to go home with a raise. The employer mounts evidence of poor work to not give a raise or leave it at a strict minimum. Why should we try to change our culture and become a more appreciative workplace? Employees – of all ages – seek appreciation from their leaders because it affirms their value within the organization and contributes to a positive workplace culture. Here are some reasons why employee appreciation is important:

- **Improved retention:** Regular recognition and appreciation can reduce turnover rates. Employees who feel valued are less likely to seek other job opportunities and more likely to feel a sense of loyalty to their employer.
- **Enhanced productivity:** Appreciation can boost morale and motivation, which can increase productivity. When employees feel their efforts are recognised, they often work harder and more efficiently. They literally go the extra mile!
- **Strengthened workplace morale:** A culture of appreciation can enhance relationships among team members and between employees and management. It fosters a sense of teamwork, and collaboration. It creates a strong

work morale in which people continue to do what they are good at, as they are praised for that.
- **Reputation:** Companies known for valuing and appreciating their employees often enjoy a better reputation, which can attract top talent and even affect customer satisfaction.
- **Overall well-being:** Receiving appreciation can improve employees' mental health by reducing stress and burnout. It helps individuals feel secure in their roles and reduces the anxiety associated with job performance.
- **Enhancing company values:** Values are not just words on paper or written on company walls; they come to life in everyday small gestures and acts of kindness. Appreciation that aligns with company values reinforces those values within the workforce, encouraging employees to embody these ideals in their daily work.

Employee appreciation is not just about the occasional thank-you note or annual award; it's about creating an environment where employees consistently feel seen, valued, and motivated to contribute their best to the organization. How can you create an appreciative culture?
- **Instil a positive culture:** Celebrate small and big successes! You know you are on a long-term journey and even if you have your big goals, don't forget to celebrate together the small steps forward! A simple compliment can make someone's day. Other ideas can be to celebrate work anniversaries, project completions, and personal milestones. This creates moments of connection and reinforces the value of individuals and their contributions.
- **Mutual feed-forward sessions:** These can be a step towards a more appreciative culture. In many evaluation meetings and feedback sessions, most of the time is spent on what went wrong, what things the employee did not achieve yet, etc. In short, it drags a lot of negative energy and is often a base for withholding a raise in salary. This is such a wasted opportunity as feed-forward sessions are positive, constructive meetings that focus on future improvement! Instead of talking mostly about what went wrong, it helps both leaders and employees to focus on how to make progress and go forward. By focusing on potential, it empowers individuals to develop their skills and capabilities. It's rooted in the belief that people can change and grow! It is a highly motivational moment. It reduces defensiveness and the frequent blaming of others. It encourages development. Why are they called mutual feed-forward

sessions? Because the best results are attained if employees are also allowed to suggest improvements to their leaders. Assessments are mutual and go in both directions! This demands preparation from both parties and let's be honest, leaders can also learn how to lead better, right? It can foster positive and equal relationships in a team and drop old hierarchical attitudes and power that one has over the other. True psychological safety is when people's ideas are heard and received without judgment or negativity.

- **Walk the talk:** As mentioned before, appreciation is like everything else in leadership; it needs to come from the top. Your behaviour sets the tone for the rest of the organization.
- **Visualise your objectives:** One of my clients has visualised their year objectives by installing champagne bottles in the corridor with the names written on them of the prospects they want to win. It reminds everyone on a daily basis what clients the sales team is chasing. It is a very simple but effective way to involve other departments in the sales objectives of the organization. Of course, when they win a prospect, the bottle is shared with the team! A great way to celebrate the hard work and milestone.
- **Transparent communication:** Foster an environment where communication is transparent and inclusive. Ensure that employees are informed and feel valued for their input and ideas. Be open to personalisation as some people may prefer public recognition, while others might value a private thank-you note or a small, thoughtful gift.
- **Training and development:** As said before, the needs of different generations vary, and cultural changes and societal trends evolve non-stop. Stay on top of your game by investing in training that helps employees develop not only their skills but also their ability to show appreciation and give positive feedback to others. Embed appreciation into the core values of the company and communicate these values clearly to all employees. Align policies and behaviours with these values.

Creating an appreciative culture is an ongoing process that requires consistency and genuine commitment. It can significantly impact employee morale, engagement, and retention, contributing to a positive workplace atmosphere and better overall performance. It is a trial-and-error process, because in an era of woke it is not always easy to give a compliment in the right way, but if it comes from an honest and authentic intention, you will for sure reap the benefits!

STEP 20: EQUALITY

This leads me to the twentieth and final step of the CARE leadership model! Congratulations, you have made it till the end, that is awesome! I promise you this last step is easier than the steps before because we can all relate to this. Nobody wants to feel that we matter less, right? We all want to be seen, be respected, and be treated as equals, right? It is just the basics of human psychology, social dynamics, and Principles of fairness and respect. Feeling appreciated and treated as an equal contribute to a positive work culture and are likely to improve both individual performance and organizational outcomes. Stimulating equality in leadership involves both structural changes within an organization and shifts in mindset among its leaders. How can you really instil equality in your processes, culture, and daily habits? Here are some strategies to foster equality:

- **Encourage open communication:** Create regular opportunities for team members to share thoughts, concerns, and ideas. This could be through regular team meetings, one-on-one check-ins, and anonymous feedback channels. Installing a post box in which employees can leave anonymous suggestions on how to make things better is a great way to ensure that everyone has a chance to speak up. When the process is not anonymous, pay attention to who is speaking up and who is not. Encourage participation from those who tend to be quieter and the introverts; particularly in digital meetings, the extroverts and loudest people easily take over. Consider structuring meetings to give everyone a chance to contribute.
- **Reduce hierarchy:** I questioned before the habit of giving the best parking spots and better catering options to the C-level, but in small gestures you can also reduce hierarchy. In meetings, it is still a habit to ask for feedback from the youngest or most junior team member first. The boss is always the last to answer. Not only does this give stress to the junior, but it also shows the unofficial ranking of people in the team, even in flat organizations. Stop doing that and randomly ask people for feedback.
- **Hire diverse people:** There is no better way to show that everyone matters than by making your team a diverse mix of talent. Actively working to create diversity at all levels, including leadership, through recruitment, promotion, and succession planning will eliminate many biases and barriers.

- **Radical transparency:** Leave no room for guessing, as that will lead to people filling in the blanks. Implement clear and transparent processes for decision-making, promotion, and compensation that are based on merit and contribution rather than seniority or other biased criteria. Dare to share the good, the bad, and the ugly. People are not stupid; by involving everyone in what goes well, and what not, you create not only a feeling of equality, but also of shared responsibility.
- **Debias systems:** Years ago, I was attending a start-up that trained AI systems. I was in shock when they showed us how biased systems like Google Image still were. But also, for instance, how a sensor under a water tap would not work when a black hand is held under it. Progress has been made since them, but vigilance remains necessary to use tools and systems that help to identify and remove bias, for instance, from job ads, evaluations, feedback, and other processes where subjective judgments may inadvertently promote inequality.

With no further ado, I was in awe of interviewing Professor Anita Nowak. Please read a short recap of her empathy insights, or simply scan the QR code below to listen to the CARE Principles podcast interview.

PODCAST INTERVIEW

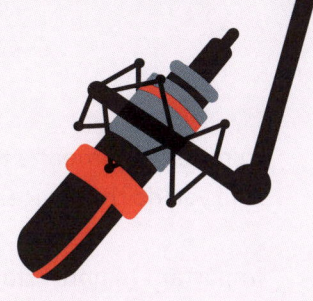

WITH PROFESSOR ANITA NOWAK, AWARD-WINNING EDUCATOR AT MCGILL UNIVERSITY CANADA

Anita Nowak is a renowned empathy expert and awarded educator, celebrated for her profound contributions to the fields of social innovation and leadership development. Anita has dedicated her academic career to understanding and teaching the transformative power of empathy in both personal and professional settings. Her innovative approach to education, combined with her dynamic public speaking and consulting, has empowered countless individuals and organizations to cultivate empathy-driven cultures. Anita's work not only enhances emotional intelligence but also drives meaningful social change, making her a pivotal figure in the movement towards more compassionate and inclusive communities.

> **There's enough research that shows that when you have empathic leadership and empathic cultures, you outperform your peers.'**
>
> **ANITA NOWAK, EMPATHY EVANGELIST**

Anita Nowak's leadership tip is an exercise: the 5 by 5. An exercise to be done with your partner, or your colleagues. It is a five-minute intervals exercise that one does five times. You sit with your partner or a colleague. The first five minutes is devoted to sitting with each other in silence. You can gaze at each other if you want, or you can close your eyes, but it's to bring stillness, it's to bring mindfulness to this container of the 5 by 5. So, you sit in silence for five minutes, and it will ground you. Then the next 20 minutes is broken into four parts of five minutes of someone talking, and someone listening. Then you change order. And you do that twice.

Important to understand that it's not a conversation! It is not about somebody speaking for five minutes, and then somebody responding to that during five minutes. It's five minutes of sharing how you are feeling. It is not about this is what happened in my day. Let me just, you know, get you up to speed on what's going on in my life. It is what one was feeling. And it's about really honouring and communicating your emotions.

Once somebody has shared for five minutes, then the next person shares for five minutes. But again, it's not about responding. So, in total, do this twice. The whole container is 25 minutes. And then when the 25 minutes are done, you don't have any conversation about what you just shared, you just move on with your day. This practice of 5 by 5 is an opportunity, a very intentional opportunity, to prioritise feelings so that you become aware of how you're feeling, and to express feelings with one another in such a way that we again are reminded that, 'Oh, you are human, too.' This practice reminds you that 'Oh, yeah, you're going through something similar too.' It just softens us.

https://spotifyanchor-web.app.link/e/XN8fLGBtgMb

EMPATHY EXERCISES

Introspection: DRAW THE HAND[115]

Solo exercise
Hand exercise: Draw your hand on paper. Write down at each finger:
Thumb: What are you good at? Did you get confirmation of this from the outside world?
Index finger: What is your future direction? Where do you want to go? What is your dream?
Middle finger: What do you hate the most? To what do you like to say 'fuck you', if you are honest with yourself?
Ring finger: To whom or to what do you want to connect?
Little finger: What progress can you make, what learning curve do you need? With the insights you have just gained, what concrete steps can you take to grow?

Purpose of this exercise: This is a reflection exercise of yourself today with your strength and better understanding of your self-knowledge. But it is also a definition of your dream and future direction. This exercise can be done on an individual level or shared with a group. It is a great idea to repeat this exercise every six months to see the progress / growth of both the individuals and the whole team.

Engagement: FROM CIRCLE TO SQUARE

Group exercise
Materials needed: A long rope tied at the ends to make a circle, blindfolds for all participants.
- Have the team stand in a circle holding the rope.
- Once everyone is holding the rope, instruct them to put on their blindfolds.
- The team's task is to form a perfect square with the rope without removing their blindfolds.
- Once they think they've formed a square, they can remove their blindfolds and see the result.

Purpose of this exercise: to reflect on the teamwork and communication strategies used and how adjustments could be made for better outcomes.

Active listening: LISTEN WITH YOUR HEART

Duo exercise
This exercise is a variant of the 5 by 5 exercise explained by Anita Nowak in the podcast.

Sit across from a colleague. For two minutes, the 'speaker' says what is on their heart; the 'listener' cannot intervene or say anything. They just listen actively and are aware of any non-verbal signals and communication cues. After two minutes, you take a one-minute break in which nobody talks. The listener gives back to the teller what they understood in essence. No reproduction of the story, but an interpretation of what seemed the most important for the teller. Make sure you really look for the non-verbal signals to capture the complete story. Then switch turns.

Purpose of this exercise: Learn active listening without interfering, without judgment, without answers, without solutions – just listening and understanding the depth of the story. Experience the power of connection while listening in silence.

Appreciation: SPREAD GOOD VIBES

Solo exercise
On a random day – not on World Compliment Day – think about the positive things your colleagues or team members have done. Write something very specific and personal for each person on a post-it and place it on their desk. If you like, you can make this anonymous or not, the choice is yours. Wait for their reactions.

Purpose of the exercise: Spread positive energy and appreciation for small daily acts of kindness. This will create a caring culture in which people feel appreciated.

Equality: LABELLING CHALLENGE

Team exercise
On post-it notes, write five things you would like to hear about yourself – things you wish others would say about you. Also, write five post-its with things you wouldn't like to hear about yourself.
Walk around the room and stick all the post-it notes on the backs of your team members. Once all the post-it notes are distributed, pair up and exchange the stacks. Take turns reading the post-it notes aloud to each other. 'Someone says about you...' Then ask: 'Can you give a specific example where this is true?'

Purpose of the exercise: To experience that feedback is not personal. That all feedback is applicable to everyone, and you can always think of a situation where you recognise yourself (in this behaviour). Self-reflection. We are all the same.

PLAY SECTION 9

THERE IS NO CARE WITHOUT SELF-CARE – A FINAL WORD ON HOW TRANSFORMATION STARTS WITHIN

To end this book, I must share a very personal story with you. A story of self-care and my years-long rejection of listening to my own intuition and gut feeling. I share this story in the hope of inspiring you to listen more carefully to your body, and not neglect it like I did for 8 years in a row! Since 2016, I suffered from a gut disease that frankly often disabled me from both work and pleasure. My gut dominated my life and prevented me from freely enjoying a meal in a restaurant, or having enough energy to simply get out of my bed. I suffer from 'leaky gut disorder'; a malfunctioning of my intestines. A disease still not officially recognised by the Western medical world.

For those who have never heard of it, think of your gut as a wall made up of tiny bricks. These bricks – or cells – are supposed to stick together tightly, forming a strong barrier that keeps bad stuff out of your bloodstream. But in people with leaky gut disorder like me, those 'bricks' become loose or damaged, creating gaps in the wall. When this happens, things that shouldn't get through, like toxins, bacteria, and undigested food particles, can slip through those gaps and enter the bloodstream. This triggers your immune system, which goes into overdrive trying to fight off these invaders. As a result, my body starts to attack itself and reacts like I have severe food poisoning. In my case, it starts with a serious migraine, soon followed by all food that needs to get out – north and south – to say it in a polite way! For as long as three days in a row, I cannot eat – even a sip of water is rejected immediately and throwing up bile is all my body does. So basically, leaky gut disorder is like having a holey wall in your gut, which lets the bad stuff sneak through and wreak havoc on your body. When I go through one of these poisonings, I have zero energy left, and the only thing to do is sleep and stay flat in my bed for a couple of days, before I can start to pick up my life where I left it.

I have always been healthy. I was lucky to be born with a large dose of energy and anything my brain conceived of doing, my body always followed. That is how I spent my life till 2016. My body felt like a separate part of me that was entirely steerable from my mind. When I started having these food poisoning experiences, I didn't think much of it at first. I blamed the meals I had. As these poisonings started to happen more frequently, I went to the doctor. The doctor had no clue and ran some allergy tests. I was not allergic to anything. Then I explored alternative healers; I was advised about a whole list of foods to avoid, and it is true that gluten, for instance – although I am not allergic to it – does trigger my gut in a negative way. But for years no real cause nor successful treatment was found.

I always thought the causes were beyond my control. I spent a fortune on doctors and treatments, impatiently waiting for a miracle pill or treatment. After each visit, treatment or blood analysis, the response from doctors was to bluntly tell me that my condition was not officially recognised by the Western medical world, so there was no real treatment. Or I received a tremendous number of supplements to take, or food to ignore. I even tried the weirdest experiences with several alternative healers, but none of their advice ever gave real relief. All the doctors always asked me how my mental health was and if I was stressed. I always replied with the same answer: sure, I had stress – who doesn't? – but it never felt so bad that it would manifest itself in my gut. In 2023, both my mental and physical health deteriorated fast.

The regular food poisonings I suffered from, lesser-known menopause effects, work and financial stress, conflicts with people I loved, and mourning the loss of both my parents turned into an explosive cocktail inside my body that exploded. I found myself in bed – impossible to even stand on my feet – for several days a month. I entirely lost my natural energy and my optimistic mood. After an entire weekend of crying, I decided to pick myself up and ask for help. I visited an alternative healer and went to see a psychologist. The healer explained to me that my intestines were not sick. My leaky gut issue was caused by a badly functioning pancreas. Because of stress, my pancreas did not make enough digestive enzymes. Food cannot be digested without these enzymes, so my intestines 'leaked' it into my blood, causing the horrible poisonings. Since this diagnosis – that was never made before, not even in university hospitals by gut specialists – I have taken natural digestive enzymes and I haven't been ill since! For details on these enzymes, please check my thank you below; I share who and what saved me!

This was a total game-changer for me, but I knew I needed to dig deeper and also look at my stress levels and mental health. I needed to dive into myself and start to listen to what my body was trying to tell me. I started a journey – with many ups and downs – of applying my CARE Principles to myself. I tried to be kinder to myself. I accepted that I did suffer from stress, something I ignored for years as I was convinced that as I love my job, I was immune to stress. Nonsense, of course, but it took me years to accept that stress not only gave me adrenaline, but also affected my physical and mental health. Combine stress with grief and getting older, and I witnessed a cocktail I could no longer ignore.

Being an independent myself for almost two decades now, I know what it feels like when my gut issue forced me to stay in bed, leaving me without a drop of energy, while I needed to work. It takes a lot for most people to stay in bed, but for independents, it has a direct effect on your revenue. The pain is double: you not only feel sick – mentally or physically – but you lose a part of your income, which also causes financial stress and even more anxiety, creating a vicious circle that is difficult to break. Without claiming that this helps with other diseases, accepting that mind and body are connected and that they influence one another was a first good step in introspection for me.

But I realised more. I saw that some choices I had made in my life went against much of my own values and norms. For years I was blind to my own moral compass, and followed a path of success that wasn't mine. I chased money, appraisal by the business world, more clients than I could handle and more revenue than was healthy for myself. For all those years, I liked to live in the 'work hard, play hard' mode, and I completely ignored all the signals my body was giving me. And believe me, those signals were brutally there, but I kind of lived in my head only, and I completely ignored my body. Sure, I practised sports, took plenty of holidays and always ate healthily. But that didn't mean that I was truly connected with myself.

Erik-Jan Mares rightfully says in the podcast: 'If you ask someone "How are you?", you should really ask "How does your body do?" because the body always indicates how you are.' Such a wise insight, but I neglected it for many years. Another thing I learned from my psychologist is that I always thought that my worries, stress, pain, and grief were minimal. I had no reason to complain, as so many others were far worse off than myself. My psychologist taught me that whatever burden you feel has a right to be there. It required serious introspection to get to the point where I am today.

With a lot of scepticism, I started a mix of stress-relief activities for more balanced health, such as sport, yoga, deep-breathing, cold showers, eating more vegan food, meditation, hypnotherapy, and psychotherapy. I must admit that since I have been practising all of the above on a regular basis, I have more control over my stress, the main cause of my leaky gut. Together with the digestive enzymes, I feel I have my energy levels back and, most importantly, my good mood. But this self-care did not come naturally to me! Going from many years of ignoring my body's signals, and believing the cause and solution were not my responsibility, I finally embraced introspection, and I rediscovered my own values and norms. I found my true purpose and am back at writing my life story. I feel happier, more balanced and believe I am again a more balanced person, both in my personal and business relationships. I finally understood how to work in full alignment of my intuition and moral compass. I need to remain vigilant as my gut is not really cured, so whenever I feel high levels of stress again, my sensitive gut warns me by playing up. It will probably be my weak spot for the rest of my life, but I now consider it my inner alarm clock telling me to slow down.

I share this personal story because I learnt the hard way that you can stimulate your health, happiness and overall well-being with less stress, enough sleep, mindfulness, love, good friends, and healthy food. How introspection can work for you will be very different than for me, but trying not to blame or change others is a good start. Transformational processes and embracing lifelong learning start within, by being curious about yourself. Be kind to yourself when you go through the journey and do not only focus on your life goals. Falling down is okay; I learnt most from my darkest moments. I got back up on my feet by accepting that I had fallen, by accepting my many flaws and failures. I am happy that my journey is what it is, as it has brought me closer to myself. The CARE Principles absolutely start with self-care and self-love.

I can only encourage you to take time for yourself in whatever form fits you best, in the hope that it will help you to find your purpose and happiness in life. I need to thank many people who came on my transformational path! In the next chapter, you will find most of them. I decided to end this chapter with a podcast interview with Matthias Lauwers.

PODCAST INTERVIEW

WITH MATTHIAS LAUWERS, YOGA TEACHER

The name Matthias Lauwers might not a ring a bell, because he is not an entrepreneur, nor a famous CEO. But he is important to me as he taught me so much about myself over the past year. Matthias studied English literature and poetry at university and is an English teacher in high school today. Matthias is also a yoga teacher and so much more to me! Matthias helps me to calm down and brings me wisdom on why we are meant to be human beings, and not human doings. Please listen to the full episode with Matthias simply by scanning the QR code below. His English accent is so nice, and his wisdom is so deep!

We are still human beings, not human doings.

MATTHIAS LAUWERS, YOGA TEACHER

Self-care tips from Matthias:
- TIP 1: I would say become very curious and nourish your body in all the ways that you can imagine or that are available to you, right? Start in a slow way. It'll take you all the way. And if we first take in healthy food, we take ample rests after a day of doing.
- TIP 2: We also take time to be a human being and already that will make a very big difference.

https://spotifyanchor-web.app.link/e/u6KjmIBtgMb

THANK YOU

This book is dedicated to my grandfather, who must have spotted my gift decades before I did.

I am grateful to my parents, who raised me in an unconventional way to live my life to the fullest and with self-confidence.

I also dedicate this book to my daughters Lua and Rocky, whom I hope to have given the right amount of love and trust to take the lead in their own lives. They also inspired me to make the right choices for them, doing my utmost to give them a positive future. They helped me to start to focus on the ecosystem we all live in. They are both wonderful Generation Z girls, a generation I admire and love for how they kick our butts and make us wake up to the world's reality! Thank you, girls!

I couldn't have written this book without the love, support, and belief in me from my boyfriend Rob. He is truly the one in our family who is the grounded foundation on which my daughters and I thrive! In my darkest moments, he comforted me to take time to heal, assuring me he would take care of all the rest. Knowing he was there helped me more than he imagines! Love you, Rob!

A special mention to my sister Ann, with whom I became very close since the passing of our parents. We have spent hours on the phone, talking about what our parents meant to us, how they influenced our lives – in positive and negative ways – and this has helped me get over my grief. I still miss my parents – my voice still cracks when I mention my mom – but I have been able to give it a place in my life. I wish that you all could have a sister like mine!

My closest friends Hilde, Véronique, Ingrid, Kathy and Charlotte keep my feet on the ground. My mentors Alexandre and Gerard are long-time supporters and caring leaders who have guided me in becoming a better version of myself.

Special thanks to Jos Rath, Theo Schuyt, Rene Repko and Henry Robben who were among the first to see the potential of the CARE Principles, and who were kind enough to open their network to me. It changed my destiny and made me understand how we can all have a positive impact and butterfly effect on the lives of others. One person can truly change the life of another. Please think about that; simply by being kind to others, and showing you care can really help them!

This book could not have been written in its current form without the tremendous help of Mette Visser. As mentioned before, Mette too was a fan from the very beginning. But to go from being an enthusiastic coach for my CARE framework, to dedicating time, energy, knowledge, and input for this book is an effort and a level of care that I could not have dreamed of. Mette is one of these people who came onto my path, and who not only has taught me so much, but has given me the confidence to collaborate full-heartedly again with others. Many exercises found in this book are inspired by Mette's leadership teachers like Alan Seale and Katie Byron.

This book is finally a testament to those who helped me shape my transformational journey:
- My amazing clients who trust me from the first eye contact and who are not afraid to work with a solo strategist.
- Xander, Matthias, and Laurenz who made me realise how physical and mental health go hand in hand.
- Applause for Hans, Marie, and Rik at ivox.be who crafted the CARE Scan, a useful analytical tool to kickstart your CARE Principles transformational journey.
- All my podcast guests, who often have never heard of me but who dare to open their hearts and businesses and share the most amazing insights with me.
- Godelieve, Ken, Koen, and Dave are my podcast allies who have helped me realise my dream to start a podcast.

- My publishing house, starting with Niels Janssens who has that amazing analytical quality of going straight to the core of the CARE Principles. I must admit that though I am sharp about my client's issues, I am hopeless at focusing on my own concept. Niels kept me sharp and focused. Thank you for that, Niels; it made a world of difference! But a good publishing house relies on more talent, so thumbs up to Marije Roefs, my editor, Anna Rich the text editor, Doriane Spans and Cami Vanstapel who helped on all other levels to publish and promote this book.
- Essentiel Antwerp and Inge Onsea who make me look fashionable and self-confident on stage and in podcast episodes. Their system of lending me their latest collections is a great way for me to look good and different for each public appearance, without breaking the bank, or over-polluting the planet.
- My health got back into shape with the help of Rick Vermuyten. He made the pancreas diagnosis, which was a first step in my healing process: https://rikvermuyten.online.
- Pharmacists Sollie in Antwerp gave me the right supplement of digestive enzymes: https://www.sollie.be.
- The enzymes that I take are called Ultra Enzymes, from the Belgian company Alfa: https://www.alfa.be/en. These enzymes literally saved my life.

Finally, I am grateful for the many friends I didn't mention, fans, followers, and acquaintances who expressed their support of the CARE Principles.
Thank you for caring! Thank you for spreading care and growing the movement!

Take care,
Isabel

Thecareprinciples.com
https://www.linkedin.com/in/isabel-verstraete-54a63b5/
https://podcasters.spotify.com/pod/show/thecareprinciples
https://www.instagram.com/isabelverstraete

ABOUT ISABEL VERSTRAETE

LEADERSHIP STRATEGIST, KEYNOTE SPEAKER, AUTHOR, AND PODCAST HOST.

Isabel is a multifaceted growth strategist who helps organizations throughout Europe grow with purpose, care and clarity. Her 20-step CARE Principles Leadership guide helps leaders create more engagement with diverse and multigenerational teams, and find sustainable growth as a result. Her clients range from multinationals to start-ups in all sectors within Europe. Renowned universities such as Vlerick, Nyenrode Business University, and VU University in Amsterdam regularly welcome Verstraete as a guest lecturer, where she shares her transformative insights rooted in the CARE Principles, leaving a lasting impact on the minds of tomorrow's leaders.

Isabel can also be booked as keynote speaker, simply contact Speakersbase for all speaking inquiries.

https://click.lannoo.be/isabel-verstraete

END NOTES

1. https://youtu.be/ODti1POj86A?si=WC7mm74t8v7K1Nlc
2. https://www.tijd.be/tablet/newspaper/vooraan/bedrijven-zonder-burn-outs-maken-40-procent-meer-winst/10533331
3. https://www.gallup.com/workplace/349484/state-of-the-global-workplace.aspx?thank-you-report-form=1
4. https://www.gallup.com/workplace/349484/state-of-the-global-workplace.aspx?thank-you-report-form=1
5. https://pminsight.cipd.co.uk/quiet-quitting-the-true-cost-of-disengaged-employees
6. https://www2.deloitte.com/us/en/insights/topics/marketing-and-sales-operations/global-marketing-trends/2020/purpose-driven-companies.html
7. https://engageforgood.com/guides/statistics-every-cause-marketer-should-know/
8. https://www.joinblink.com/intelligence/employee-engagement-statistics
9. https://www.metmette.nl/bio
10. https://bronnieware.com/blog/regrets-of-the-dying/
11. https://podcasters.spotify.com/pod/show/thecareprinciples
12. https://podcasts.apple.com/be/podcast/grow-your-brands-impact-with-the-care-principles/id1555931557?l=nl
13. https://study.com/academy/lesson/bureaucracy-max-webers-theory-of-impersonal- https://www.mindtools.com/anx8725/frederick-taylor-and-scientific-management
14. https://www.gallup.com/home.aspx
15. https://www.academia.edu/44861150/Leadership_In_Pursuit_of_Purpose
16. https://youtu.be/Nno1faLhoWk?si=dZyMGPll4qC8IkW-

17 Peter Dizikes: "Thomas Friedman examines impact of global 'accelerations'", MIT News (2018), bit.ly/2KuNLwh.
18 https://news.gallup.com/poll/506765/social-conservatism-highest-decade.aspx
19 https://www.standaard.be/cnt/dmf20240206_97875015
20 https://www.gallup.com/home.aspx
21 https://www.gallup.com/workplace/610856/new-challenge-engaging-younger-workers.aspx
22 https://www.investopedia.com/what-is-quiet-quitting-6743910
23 https://www.lse.ac.uk/News/Latest-news-from-LSE/2023/f-June-2023/Widespread-evidence-of-'quiet-quitting'-in-the-UK-labour-market
24 https://finance.yahoo.com/news/bare-minimum-monday-latest-workplace-141234469.html?guccounter=1
25 https://www.ucl.ac.uk/news/2023/mar/analysis-remote-working-how-surge-digital-nomads-pricing-out-local-communities-worldwide
26 https://www.wellandgood.com/polyworking/
27 https://socialscienceandhumanities.ontariotechu.ca/workplacebullying/power-control-wheel.php
28 https://www.cnbc.com/2022/10/08/psychologist-ronald-riggio-why-people-follow-toxic-bosses.html#:~:text=People%20can't%20always%20know,trying%20to%20reap%20personal%20benefits
29 https://www.fish-tales.com/
30 https://www.amazon.com.be/-/en/William-Strauss/dp/0767900464
31 https://youtu.be/1QnilLfex7A?si=zGL5vNvAVdfw6H6Y
32 https://action.deloitte.com/insight/3755/workplace-worries-create-barriers-to-the-authentic-self
33 https://hr-on.com/en/
34 https://dictionary.cambridge.org/dictionary/english/kpi: key performance indicator: a way of measuring a company's progress towards the goals it is trying to achieve
35 https://podcasters.spotify.com/pod/show/thecareprinciples/episodes/Marc-Noppen--CEO-of-the-University-Hospital-Brussels-explains-how-a-better-collaboration-helped-his-hospital-through-Covid-e182crn/a-a6k022d
36 https://www.ivox.be/

37 https://thecareprinciples.com/the-care-scan/
38 https://en.wikipedia.org/wiki/Vagus_nerve
39 https://brain.harvard.edu/hbi_news/how-the-brain-communicates-with-the-gut/
40 https://sloanreview.mit.edu/article/a-noble-purpose-alone-wont-transform-your-company/
41 https://www.ncbi.nlm.nih.gov/pmc/articles/PMC3108032/#:~:text=SUMMARY,of%20behavior%20and%20psychological%20experience.
42 https://spotifyanchor-web.app.link/e/9sXZYwVuiJb
43 https://www.frontiersin.org/journals/psychology/articles/10.3389/fpsyg.2021.675543/full
44 https://www.weforum.org/agenda/2022/11/4-ways-purpose-into-profitability/
45 https://www.clientearth.org/latest/news/we-re-joining-legal-action-against-total-for-greenwashing/
46 https://www.thepinknews.com/2023/12/06/human-rights-campaign-starbucks-inclusion-award-unions/
47 https://en.wikipedia.org/wiki/Pareto_principle
48 https://www.lerenloslaten.com/jan-bommerez/
49 https://news.uchicago.edu/story/mihaly-csikszentmihalyi-pioneering-psychologist-and-father-flow-1934-2021
50 https://www.psychologicalscience.org/news/minds-business/being-able-to-personalize-your-workspace-may-have-psychological-benefits.html
51 https://www.weforum.org/agenda/2018/11/open-plan-offices-make-workers-less-collaborative-harvard-study-finds/#:~:text=URL%3A%20https%3A%2F%2Fwww.weforum.org%2Fagenda%2F2018%2F11%2Fopen
52 https://psychology.stanford.edu/people/carol-dweck
53 https://cifs.dk/p/digital-the-future-of-workplace-strategy
54 https://podcasts.apple.com/fr/podcast/hoe-cre%C3%ABer-je-duurzame-groei-in-een-dalende-markt-de/id1555931557?i=1000542810676
55 https://www.corporate-rebels.com/
56 https://farsight.cifs.dk/
57 https://spotifyanchor-web.app.link/e/JywmuJ7xTIb
58 https://youtu.be/TNdGzGmnlL8?si=OwpCkdpglzsyBWfR

59 https://www.perspectivesllc.com/results-focused-v-people-focused-leadership/
60 https://claude.ai
61 https://www2.deloitte.com/content/dam/Deloitte/mt/Documents/about-deloitte/deloitte-2023-genz-millennial-survey-mental-health.pdf
62 https://www.who.int/news-room/fact-sheets/detail/mental-health-at-work
63 https://www.stress.org/stress-research
64 https://www.pcbb.com/bid/2022-03-30-mitigating-employee-stress-for-higher-productivity
65 https://www.gallup.com/workplace/351545/great-resignation-really-great-discontent.aspx
66 https://medium.com/@benjamin_goss/the-silent-epidemic-employee-burnout-in-2023-2b40627100bf
67 https://www.who.int/news-room/fact-sheets/detail/adolescent-mental-health
68 https://www.statista.com/statistics/1400861/percentage-of-individuals-reporting-symptoms-of-stress-depression-anxiety-by-age-group-worldwide/
69 https://www.betterup.com/
70 https://helloezra.com/
71 https://thrivepartners.co.uk/
72 https://www.netflix.com/be/title/81133260
73 https://en.fuckupnights.com/
74 https://corpgov.law.harvard.edu/2023/02/22/gender-diversity-in-the-c-suite/
75 https://www.fastcompany.com/section/innovation-festival-360
76 https://www.theguardian.com/sustainable-business/2016/jun/08/workplace-gender-equality-invisible-privilege
77 https://hbr.org/2015/11/ceos-with-daughters-run-more-socially-responsible-firms
78 https://www.independent.co.uk/travel/news-and-advice/denmark-more-mythical-statues-than-women-copenhagen-b2509282.html
79 https://spotifyanchor-web.app.link/e/5xIZwiTNSHb
80 https://www.pewresearch.org/social-trends/2023/03/01/the-enduring-grip-of-the-gender-pay-gap/

81 https://www.antwerppride.com/
82 https://desingel.be/nl/programma/dans/vogue-bootcamp-belgium-the-abundance-ball
83 https://www.netflix.com/be/title/80241986
84 https://eu.usatoday.com/story/money/2023/05/18/bud-light-loses-lgbtq-score-after-dylan-mulvaney-transgender-campaign/70229893007/
85 https://thehill.com/homenews/state-watch/4134358-king-of-beers-no-more-how-bud-light-lost-its-crown/
86 https://www.shrm.org/
87 https://www.tomwujec.com/marshmallow-challenge
88 https://www.edelman.be/research/edelman-trust-barometer-2020
89 https://www.accenture.com/_acnmedia/pdf-109/accenture-ungc-ceo-study.pdf
90 https://www.globalgoals.org/
91 https://commercial.cnn.com/why-trust-relevance-reliability-matters-news-consumers
92 https://en.wikipedia.org/wiki/Reality_tunnel
93 https://www.edelman.com/trust/2024/Trust-Barometer/innovation-trust-test-business
94 https://hbr.org/2022/11/how-bullying-manifests-at-work-and-how-to-stop-it
95 https://www.brookings.edu/people/richard-v-reeves/
96 https://www.atlassian.com/company
97 https://wtop.com/business-finance/2020/04/hilton-donates-1m-room-nights-to-front-line-medical-workers/
98 https://brenebrown.com/
99 https://www.youtube.com/watch?v=iCvmsMzlF7o
100 https://www.bamementalhealth.org/post/four-attributes-of-empathy-dr-teresa-wiseman
101 https://www.ncbi.nlm.nih.gov/pmc/articles/PMC9486696/#:~:text=Scientific%20evidence%20has%20consistently%20shown,%5D%2C%20%5B10%5D%5D.
102 https://www.businessolver.com/
103 https://www.bol.com/be/nl/f/verslaafd-aan-ons-eigen-gelijk/9300000145271670/

END NOTES

104 https://www.ft.com/content/0e2f6f8e-bb03-4fa7-8864-f48f576167d2
105 https://hbr.org/2018/11/how-masculinity-contests-undermine-organizations-and-what-to-do-about-it?registration=success
106 https://www.businessolver.com/
107 https://www.ocregister.com/2024/04/23/tesla-layoffs-draw-suit-claiming-not-enough-warning-for-workers/
108 https://www.wired.com/story/google-meta-big-tech-is-bad-at-firing/
109 https://www.gallup.com/workplace/349484/state-of-the-global-workplace.aspx?thank-you-report-form=1
110 https://www.gsb.stanford.edu/insights/david-larcker-lonely-top-resonates-most-ceos
111 https://youtu.be/QlmlqAWocUQ?si=tO7ci9ahO9Dq4ByZ
112 https://www.consilium.europa.eu/en/policies/mental-health/#:~:text=The%20state%20of%20mental%20health%20in%20the%20EU,-Before%20the%20COVID&text=Anxiety%20disorders%20affected%20an%20estimated,11%20million%20people%2C%202.4%25).
113 https://bmcpublichealth.biomedcentral.com/articles/10.1186/s12889-023-16797-z#:~:text=Previous%20studies%20which%20also%20used,25%2Dyear%2Dolds).
114 https://hammondpsychology.com/praise-vs-punishment/#:~:text=From%20a%20strictly%20psychological%20standpoint,you%20want%20in%20your%20children.
115 https://www.linkedin.com/in/anke-jansen/?originalSubdomain=nl

DO YOU

CARE?

D/2024/45/332 – ISBN 978 94 014 3797 4 – NUR 800

Interior design: Adept vormgeving
Cover design: Margo Togni
Translation: Isabel Verstraete
Illustrations: Lucia Biancalana

© Isabel Verstraete & Lannoo Publishers nv, Tielt, 2024.

LannooCampus Publishers is a subsidiary of Lannoo Publishers, the book and multimedia division of Lannoo Publishers nv.

All rights reserved.
No part of this publication may be reproduced and/or made public, by means of printing, photocopying, microfilm or any other means, without the prior written permission of the publisher.

LannooCampus Publishers
Vaartkom 41 box 01.02
3000 Leuven
Belgium

P.O. Box 23202
1100 DS Amsterdam
The Netherlands

www.lannoocampus.com